*All Blood Is Red . . .*
*All Shadows Are Dark!*

January 24, 1986

To Jim and Margot,
  Special, caring people.
With best wishes from
the Becker family.
        Stanley, Tom
          Monti
        Malcolm
        Marquita
        Meredith
        Marty

*Dedicated to
Montieth
Martin
Malcolm
Meredith
Marquita,
whom we love profoundly,
who have provided the context for
this book and
who may be doing more than
children should be asked to do.*

# All blood is red...

# all shadows are dark!

**Edited by John T. and Stanli K. Becker**

*Seven Shadows Press*
P.O. BOX 1118   CLEVELAND, OHIO 44120

Copyright © 1984 by John T. and Stanli K. Becker.
All rights reserved. No part of this book may be reproduced or transmitted in any form or by any means, electronic or mechanical, including photocopying, recording, or by any information storage and retrieval system, without permission in writing from the authors. Permission of the authors will be granted, without charge, to an interested person or group of persons who may wish to use "A Letter to the Teacher," Chapter 20, in whole or part. Permission will likewise be granted to those who wish to adapt "A Letter to the Teacher" to a personal or group situation. To obtain permission, write to Seven Shadows Press, P. O. Box 1118, Cleveland, OH 44120. Enclose a self-addressed, stamped envelope with the request.

Grateful acknowledgment is made to Dr. Edward S. Hope for permission to use the poem, "Call Me Human/Why Label Me?" from a collection of poems, *Glass Behind*, written by his late wife, Marion Conover Hope.

Cover design and illustrations by J. Howard Noel
Cover photograph by Steven C. Mariakis
Composition by Oberlin Printing Company

Published by Seven Shadows Press, P. O. Box 1118, Cleveland, Ohio 44120
First Printing
Printed in the United States of America
ISBN 0-916225-00-3

# Contents

| | | |
|---|---|---|
| **Preface** | | ix |
| *Tom* | | |
| **Acknowledgments** | | xiii |
| *Stanli and Tom* | | |
| **1** | America's Deep-Rooted Ways | 1 |
| | *Tom* | |
| **2** | One Black Drop | 9 |
| | *Stanli* | |
| **3** | Are You from a Home | 17 |
| | *Tom* | |
| **4** | Seen, Yet Unseen | 21 |
| | *Stanli* | |
| **5** | Smoke Clouds on a Desegregated Bus | 27 |
| | *Tom* | |
| **6** | Mirror Images | 37 |
| | *Stanli* | |
| **7** | Reductio Ad Absurdum | 43 |
| | *Stanli* | |
| **8** | Music Has a Color Line, Too | 53 |
| | *Martin* | |
| **9** | Race-Thinking | 55 |
| | *Stanli* | |
| **10** | Where's Your Mommy | 63 |
| | *Meredith* | |
| **11** | The White Grandmother | 65 |
| | *Tom* | |
| **12** | I Can't Wait | 69 |
| | *Marquita* | |

| | | |
|---|---|---|
| **13** | Pink-White Daddy and Brown-Black Son<br>*Malcolm* | 71 |
| **14** | Blackness and Reality<br>*Stanli* | 75 |
| **15** | Call Me Human<br>*Tom* | 87 |
| **16** | Computers Don't Take Human<br>*Tom* | 91 |
| **17** | The Marshal Never Came<br>*Montieth* | 99 |
| **18** | They Don't Count Me<br>*Martin* | 103 |
| **19** | Mixed Origins<br>*Stanli* | 107 |
| **20** | A Letter to the Teacher<br>*Stanli and Tom* | 117 |
| **21** | What Natural Parting<br>*Tom* | 121 |
| **22** | Why Bus Me<br>*Montieth* | 131 |
| **23** | To Kill a Myth<br>*Stanli and Tom* | 135 |

Epilogue   141
*Stanli*

Notes   145

Index   151

*I am white and I am black, and know that there is no difference. Each casts a shadow, and all shadows are dark.*

**Walter White**
**Saturday Review of Literature**
**11 Oct., 1947, p. 52**

# *Preface*

"Hey, Monti! Monti! Wait up!" Twelve-year-old Monti turned around in the crowded, junior high school hallway to see who was calling her. A boy hurried toward her. "Hi, Monti. Can I ask you something? I keep on thinking about it. Don't get mad, okay?"

Monti shrugged her shoulders and looked at him questioningly, knowing that the bell would signal the beginning of the next class in a minute or two.

"You know, I can't figure out what color you are," he told her. "Your hair looks white, but . . ."

"My hair is brown," said Monti, tilting her head and peering down at the hair on her shoulder.

"You know what I mean," he said, uneasily.

"My hair is brown and looks brown. See?" Monti smiled at him as she toyed with a few strands of her hair.

Reluctantly, he looked at her hair. Then he asked, "Well . . . well, are you black or white? Honest to God, I can't tell."

"I'm human, just like you and everybody else." Monti chuckled slightly, gave him a broad grin and waved as the bell sounded. "I'll be late. See ya."

"It really doesn't make any difference to me," he yelled toward Monti as she headed for her next class.

This brief exchange between my daughter Monti and one of her classmates illustrates what this book is about. When young people do not automatically classify their friends as "black" or "white," when they feel the need to ask who is what race and to think about how they will know or decide, then do they disrupt that process which conditions and dehumanizes people into commonly accepted, rigid "racial" categories. The mythology of race becomes exposed as the monstrous lie that it is when a person acknowledges that neither "black" alone nor "white" alone can account for the blends of skin colors and hair textures or the shapes of noses or lips or eyes or foreheads.

Children who do explore the meanings and implications of "blackness" and "whiteness" soon discover, however, that society has allowed them no choice. They find themselves assigned as "black" or "white," regardless of their observations, explorations or desires. Their young minds are cultivated for and made susceptible to what the distinguished anthropologist Ashley Montagu calls "man's most dangerous myth" and the "witchcraft of our time."[1] That people can be divided into distinct, separate and identifiable "races" is the myth; that the human experience is or should be affected in any way by "race" is the witchcraft. The differentiation between "black" and "white," forced upon children in America, deprives them of one of the strongest principles of human growth and development—choice within reason!

This book is the work of my family. I'm the father, recognized as "white" in traditional American color-coding. My wife is called "black," even though her grahamcracker-colored skin is not purely of black African origins. When people see one or both of us with our five children, we are often mistaken for social workers who have brought a few youngsters from some kind of home or agency out for an occasion. "What a hodgepodge!" we've been called, based on our contrasting skin tones, ranging from ivory to ebony, including light pink, ecru, tan, honey and dark brown. This medley of colors is possible, in our case, both because of our "interracial" marriage and because four of our five children are adopted.

All seven of us are contributors to this book, and each

has written at least one section—even the youngest. We write with the ambitious purpose of exposing the absurdities of "race-thinking," as Jacques Barzun called it in his classic 1937 book *Race: a Study in Modern Superstition*;[2] we do so by relying more on common family experiences than on scholarly works. We parents helped each child, especially the younger ones, write about those personal incidents he or she selected as important and memorable. Each writer is identified by his or her first name at the beginning of each section.

We admit to the overuse of quotation marks to set off certain words, such as "race," "black," "white" and some others. All of us understand the conventional usages of these words and use them as the reader probably would. However, since words having to do with racial identity don't have the same meaning to us that they have to most people in America, we often place them in quotation marks. These are words which our family does not ordinarily use. In this writing, however, we set a trap for ourselves from which we have been unable to escape. That trap is our using the word "race" and the concept of "race" to mean anything other than the "human race." We become entrapped also by our own use of the terms "biracial," "interracial," "multiracial" and a few others; even these classifications are part of the problem—the pigeonholing of people into groups which should have no bearing on the quality of life or the human condition. Beyond our home, we admit to having no immediate solution for this; nevertheless, we put great effort into maintaining a constant awareness of the need to seek resolutions.

Unfortunately, as in many writings, some ideas are introduced, then skirted or oversimplified in a statement or two; in many cases, readers are referred to the Notes for additional works on these matters. We can but apologize and hope that we have effectively fastened onto the point we tried to make in the process.

Because of the overwhelming preoccupation with black-white relationships in our nation, this book is intentionally limited to discussing these. However, it should become apparent that much of what is written here pertains to other racial/ethnic family compositions. Much of the content also applies to families which have become interracial through adoption only—"whites" who adopt minority children, especially.

My wife Stanli and I had no intention of writing this book when we married seventeen years ago. This undertaking we owe to our children.

Tom<br>
(John T. Becker)<br>
June 21, 1984

# *Acknowledgments*

Recognizing fully the roles our families and friends have played in our lives, we express thanks to the whole spectrum: those who approved our marriage and those who did not; those who cautioned us or admonished; those with whom we broke and mended ties. The supporters and the detractors, in-laws and "out-laws"—all have contributed to our development. By name, some must be mentioned: the late Elsie Louise Mitchell, the late Louis P. Becker, Mary K. Lohr, George Howard Mitchell, Jan W. Mitchell, Robert E. Becker, Monteith L. Mitchell, Mary Lou and Paul Heckman, Helen McDermott, Alicia McDermott, Tia R. Mitchell, Marcenia B. Mitchell, the late Betty Goldkamp, Louis Goldkamp, Roscoe and Henrietta Swann, Virginia Hunter Harris, Michele Johnson Jones, Shiryl Johnson Nelson, Gladys W. Wilson, the late Edward "Mike" Johnson, Louis Heckman, Margaret Heckman Weimer, the late Nathaniel Mitchell, Colleen B. Mitchell, Susan Mitchell, Lawrence J. Lohr, Agneta Knall Mitchell, Otis and Charles Owens, Susan and Robert Baker and their children—Robert, Rebecca and Mark.

Through the years a number of people have shared parts of their personal lives with us. Among these, special gratitude is expressed to Selina D. Burrucker, Joseph D. Burrucker, Louise K. Hope and Dr. Edward S. Hope.

A few people read portions of the manuscript while it was being prepared and offered suggestions which brought about notable changes, additions or deletions. They are Nancy C. Butler, Robert A. Hanson, Dr. Major

L. Harris, George H. Mitchell, Jr., Dr. Rae Rohfeld and our reader, who wishes to remain anonymous.

While recognizing the contributions of others, we must, however, accept full responsibility for the ideas expressed, their selection and their presentation; we absolve all but ourselves for whatever shortcomings the reader may find.

We feel especially indebted to J. Howard Noel—cousin, friend, artist—for the layout, cover design and illustrations. In addition, we have appreciated his interest and sound advice in matters related to publication.

Finally, we are deeply obliged to the late Emily Isabelle Hamler, "Aunt Belle," whose financial support helped make this book a reality.

S. K. B./J. T. B.

# 1

## America's Deep-Rooted Ways
### by Tom

My family follows the paths well-trodden by many other families. The children attend public schools, pledge allegiance to the flag, ride bikes, sit on Santa's lap, dye Easter eggs and stand in block-long lines to ride roller coasters. My wife and I support the schools, work PTA carnival booths and bake cupcakes *ad infinitum*. We served as PTA co-president for one unforgettable year: our house caught on fire, and the PTA records went up in smoke. We parents spend endless hours with children on homework. "Straighten your rooms" and "Pick up your things" echo daily throughout our home. We mow the grass, shovel the snow, do the laundry and run innumerable errands. We chauffeur and car pool for countless activities—birthday parties, sleep-overs, school socials, hockey, baseball, soccer and swim teams, and lessons galore.

Despite our practices of these deep-rooted American ways, we are still viewed as a different kind of family. As one nearby resident told a newcomer to the community some years ago, "You haven't met the Beckers yet? You can't miss them when they're on their bikes. They are quite unique. You'll know them when you see them."

Our suburban community of tree-lined streets, carefully-wooded parks, man-made lakes and well-kept, old homes is a cyclist's haven. Like almost everyone else around here, we do have bikes; but, certainly, it's not the uniqueness of these bicycles that makes us so easily recognized. Our older children, if asked, could explain what the neighbor meant when she told the newcomer in the community, "You'll know them when you see them." As our children advance in years and venture into the neighborhood, community and beyond, they learn that a person's skin color is, indeed, a serious matter. It has become obvious to them that passers-by must expect some kind of color uniformity in family groupings. The children notice the stares, glares, gestures and comments of others, particularly when the whole family is together. We have walked by many, many people who have turned around to take one more look at our family of varied skin colors. What these people do is called a double take: they turn around and take a second, longer look. Persons with visible, physical handicaps must be accustomed to these double takes, too.

Curiosity about our lifestyle is usually generated by a physical view of the family, which often leads people to speculate that our thoughts, ideas and behaviors may also be different from those of traditional families. They are right in guessing that our philosophy may be as unusual as our composition. Our outright rejection of "race"—a viewpoint we readily share with others—is often an added reason for people to describe us as "unique," in the words of the above neighbor. That we have chosen not to follow the "racial" ideologies of American society is, in great part, the subject of this book. Our children have learned to recognize, accept and understand skin color and other physical differences among people as normal variations characteristic of one human "race," if that term must be used. We do alert and caution the children early, however, that few others may think as they do. Soon, through their personal experiences outside the home, they discover other children and adults who classify people rigidly as "black" and "white." They must grapple with the idea that others—even their friends—are taught carefully that people who are not black are "black" and that people who are not white are "white." More difficult for their young minds to grasp is that kind of "race-thinking" which holds that a light-tan skinned girl must be called "black" and learn to call herself "black," even though her skin color resembles closely the skin pigmentation of those who call themselves "white." It is downright hard for our children to comprehend why there is the need for individuals to be classified as either "black" or "white."

I recall a curious and alert child, some years ago, who tried to fit our family into these familiar patterns of "black" and "white." A nucleus of five then, we were on one of our frequent bicycle excursions through the neighborhood. We had pulled our bikes over to the curb to exchange greetings with some neighbors who were out for a stroll. We had talked for a couple of minutes, still poised on our bikes, when a little boy, perhaps five, wandered down his driveway toward us. His younger sister, about three, trailed behind him. They stopped several feet short of our two little tykes, one strapped in a kiddie carrier on the rear of Stanli's bike and the other in the carrier on mine. Monti, the oldest of our three children, rode on the sidewalk on her two-wheeler with training wheels, and she had just caught up with us. The children eyed one another carefully. Of course, that's just part of growing up and learning; kids stare at other kids. But there was more than "sizing up" on the mind of this little boy.

"Is she your mom?" he asked, looking at Martin who was then a blond, curly-haired, three-year-old tot.

Martin nodded yes.

"Yes, I'm Martin's mom," said Stanli, breaking a moment's silence.

"But you're black, and he's white." And turning to two-year-old Malcolm, seated on the back of my bike, the wide-eyed youngster pointed and said, "He's black. He should be on your bike," looking back at Stanli and pointing at her. Puzzled also by my presence as the other adult rider, he asked, "Is he a daddy?"

"Yes, he's a daddy. He's their daddy," Stanli indicated, pointing to our three children. She knew that she could not leave this child in a quandry or, for that matter, our ever curious, five-year old daughter, not to mention the observing neighbors whose faces reflected that Stanli and I might be getting what we deserved. She asked the baffled child, "Is everyone in your family the same color?"

"Unh huh," he said, his head nodding up and down in honesty befitting only childhood.

"Well, in our family we are different colors—something like crayons. There are lots of families all over the world with moms and dads and children who are different in color, just as we are. Maybe you haven't seen too many of them yet. Check your own family. See if everybody's the same color. Maybe your mom is a little pinker than you are. Or maybe your dad is a little bit rosier or yellower than your mom."

The boy studied Stanli for three or four seconds and then said, "Okay, I'll go tell my mom."

Off he went with his sister skipping and hopping behind him. Before he entered his house, he stopped and turned around to take another look. What would he tell his mother about this family of different colors? Perhaps he might even have a question or two about skin colors in his own family. It would have been interesting to monitor the exchange of ideas which was about to take place in his house.

"That was cute," said one of the neighbors halfheartedly. Her wobbly tone indicated to me that she would handle our way of thinking once we were on our separate ways.

Stanli and I pondered and talked often about how best

to handle the frank questions and observations about our family posed frequently by curious, little children. We did want to be fair to these inquisitive, still somewhat free-thinking youngsters. At the same time, we had to be fair to our own children and true to our beliefs. When Stanli asked the little boy to check members of his own family to see if there wasn't a little bit of difference in their skin colors, she was only doing what she and I had done, and still do, for our own children.

From their earliest years, our children have learned to recognize their mirror images: the complexion of their skins, the shape and color of their eyes, the texture and color of their hair. Teaching children to attend to individual differences is a first step in combatting that oversimplified process whereby people are rigidly categorized into separate and distinct groups, thus laying the foundation for stereotyped thinking and prejudiced beliefs. Children should grow up with at least the opportunity to discover that they—each of them, in his or her own way—are unique and beautiful human beings. With that as a basic assumption, we insured that our children learned from their earliest days that they are unique, beautiful and special, and that they do not fit conveniently into color-coded "racial" categories. "Black" and "white," words which are obviously not descriptive of people's actual skin colors, were not very useful in the children's early formative years, except perhaps in conversations or observations related to hair color.

Not all people who speak of "black" and "white," however, are strangers to our children; some are very close to them. At different times, the children have heard their grandparents—black Granddad and white Nana—talk about their racial identities.

Granddad Mitchell, retired Assistant Attorney General for the State of West Virginia, has spoken to them of some of his personal and professional activities to alleviate injustices and to negotiate changes to resolve racial problems. "I'm proud to be a black man. I worked and your Gran worked to make things better for black people. So did my children. I know your mom has told you about the sit-ins, those big marches, and other things she did." The children would sit hushed, while Granddad recalled these things for them. They have giggled, played and been impressed with this handsome, brown-skinned, gray-haired, not-too-often-seen relative, "Mom's Dad."

Then, there's "Dad's Mom." The children very much relish asking Nana about Dad's boyhood, the trouble he got into, and the spankings or other punishments which followed. But they also talk to their grandmother about more serious things, including her many awards and pins. A devout Catholic, Nana has been very active in both Catholic and ecumenical causes for many years, always involved in race relations as well.

"There are lots of white people who have worked for the equality of all," she has told them. "And I'm one of them. When white people are accused of doing so many awful things, I bristle some. I'm very proud of being white and standing up for what I believe and know is right." The children get fidgety when they sense a lecture forthcoming, especially on this subject. However, they know what Nana means.

Sometimes grandparents make things hard for kids. Most of the time the children are treated by their grandparents as thinking, little people who are expected to respond after listening and pondering. Yet, there are times when the children need to be silent, polite, and to listen without commenting. One such time is when their grandparents speak of themselves as being "black" or "white." It has been difficult for us, as parents, to get this point across to the children. "Old fashioned," they call it. "We have to be old fashioned for awhile today," they sometimes grumble. They think it's hilarious when Mom or Dad says, "There used to be times when children were 'seen but not heard.'" In fact, we parents have had to convince them that they, themselves, should be able to discern when it is appropriate to be silent and not comment at that moment on what is said to them. Grandparents are not the only ones who provide these occasions; so do uncles, aunts and some other relatives.

"But we can think and tell you about it later? Right, Mom?" might be the response of one of them. Or, "You'll explain to us when we're by ourselves if we ask you? Right, Dad?" We assure them that we will discuss anything they wish, and we do set time aside to do this. Our family conferences are frequent, but rarely do they last more than ten to fifteen minutes. Our children, like most youngsters, simply don't dwell on these matters for long. Seldom do these concerns linger till the next sunrise. The children sleep with dreams of tomorrow's ice cream treat of mint-chocolate chip and pink bubble gum flavors, of the weekend's fishing trip, of that Saturday baby-sitting job, or of ghosts, monsters and bizarre chases through lands never pictured on TV. Our youngest yearns for a pair of roller skates, another for his first two-wheeler, and the older ones for new hockey sticks, the latest video-game cartridges, or a portable transistor radio called a "box" or a "walkman."

Nevertheless, on the next occasion when Granddad espouses his "blackness," or Nana her "whiteness," the children will become uneasy, weigh these things thoughtfully and still have a hard time keeping quiet. The children know that Granddad knows that he isn't really "black" as crayons are black; that Nana is perfectly aware that she is not "white" as notebook paper is white. They also try to understand why both of them talk that way. Still, it is difficult for the children to subscribe to these rigid, definitive labels, "black" and "white." Moreover, the young Beckers realize that the happenstance of skin color should not be the pivotal circumstance that it is in their lives.

# 2

## *One Black Drop*
by Stanli

"Wait a minute, Tom," I said, getting up from the dining room table and walking into the living room. "You don't understand. I didn't make the rules. Blacks didn't make the rules. It's whites! White society!" By this time I had pulled the book *Simple Takes A Wife* by Langston Hughes from the bookcase and was searching for a page I knew was there.

Tom had followed right behind me. "Stanli, I don't give a damn whose rule it is! They're wrong! That's what's important! They're wrong . . . absolutely wrong!"

"Wait, honey. Just wait!" I insisted. I had found the page. "Let me read this to you. 'It's powerful . . . that one drop of Negro blood . . .'"

"Oh, come off it, Stanli," shouted Tom irately, breaking into my reading.

Even though I was becoming annoyed, I read on, "'because just *one* drop of black blood makes a man colored. One drop—you are a Negro. Black is powerful.'[3] Langston Hughes wrote this almost twenty years ago, Tom. I didn't make this up, and neither did he!"

"Don't read that stuff to me! I don't care what Langston Hughes said or, for that matter, anyone else. Monti's heritage is Irish! German, too! Not just YOUR Afro-American! What if I choose to talk about white blood? Do you think that I think so little of myself as to believe that your 'black blood' is all powerful? Well, I don't."

I was momentarily stunned by this admission Tom had just made—that he, a "white" man, actually wanted "his half" of our daughter's heritage publicly and loudly recognized after eons of "white" denial and rejection of any such claims. This was "a bit much"! How could Tom refuse to recognize the realities? "Who the hell do you think you are?" I found myself shouting. "Black blood . . . white blood—in a minute you'll be talking about your heritage and 'blue blood.' ALL BLOOD IS RED! . . . but that doesn't change the rules of a game that has been going on for over three hundred years. Don't take my word for it." I shoved the Langston Hughes book within an inch of Tom's nose. "Here, you ought to read this. You might learn something!"

I didn't note the date of that Saturday night marital dispute in 1971, but that has not lessened its impact upon our lives. Tom and I had been married almost four years on that evening. The wine, flowers and china atop our only damask tablecloth with candles flickering in the dimly lit dining room lent to an atmosphere quite different than customary at our evening meal. Conspicuous by its absence was the highchair usually placed between us, not to mention the silverware being tossed to the floor amidst the loud baby echoes of "ma-ma . . . da-da . . . hot!" The little "sugarplum," about whom we argued, had been asleep for a couple of hours when Tom and I seated ourselves at the dining room table. Having dinner alone together late at night took root early in our marriage as we sought relief and relaxation from regular routines and rigors.

This hassle over our one-year-old daughter's "racial" identity erupted midway through dinner when, for the first time, I referred to Monti as "black." We had just received an envelope from the county welfare department, containing a sheath of forms about adoption. The

"ABC—Adopt a Black Child" drive was prominently advertised on television and in newspapers. What I had said was, "Tom, when I see those pictures of other black children, like Monti, who need homes, I think it's time." Little did I realize that this quietly spoken comment would lead us into this near-midnight confrontation.

Romantic dinner? Not that night. The next morning we completed the adoption forms amidst the distractions of "da-da . . . ma-ma . . . hot!" There was no mention of that "one black drop." An uneasy truce between Tom and me reigned that Sunday. Any appeasements we made, I believe, were due to our mutual desires to move ahead with our first adoption; after all, we had talked about and agreed upon adoption even before we were married.

That heated debate marked the first time that I had been faced with the possibility that a child with "one black drop" could be considered openly to be anything other than "black." "Whites" had considered practically every child of interracial union as "black" since the 1660s when laws were enacted in Virginia and Maryland to ensure that children born of "white" women servants and "black" slaves would be called "Negroes" and, in those days, forced into slavery. The "white" plantation master rarely claimed his own offspring from his "Negro" women slaves, and these "mulatto" children were necessarily raised in the slave quarters. No matter about appearances, forget future relationships; anyone known to have "color" anywhere in his or her lineage was considered "black." "Blacks" had concurred. They, the minority, had no choice but to accommodate to the will and power of "white" America. And that's the way things have been for hundreds of years. I learned to think this way, as did my brothers, and finally my little sister.

In 1963, when my light-brown-skinned sister, at age three, announced that she was "white," horror filled other family members. We could not believe that we had gone wrong. How could this little girl with two older brothers and an older sister—all potential jailbirds because of our civil rights activities—fail to realize that she was, indeed, not "white"?

"She's thinking about crayon colors," our mother Louise said. Mama, almost "white-looking" herself, had bought that white doll last Christmas saying, "Well, she really is closer to the color of this doll than the black ones they make."

The babysitter laughed and laughed. Virginia tee-heed for what seemed like hours when three-year-old Monteith told her of her "whiteness."

"Y'all better get this child together," the sitter spat in the faces of us three older children amidst her tears, flowing from hard laughter. Near panic was my feeling and seemed to be echoed by my brothers. I was 19 years old and actively participating in the civil rights struggles of the early sixties—boycotting, marching, registering potential voters, standing-in at movie theatres and sitting-in at lunch counters. Yes, this darling, little, longed-for sister was sugar-cookie tan and had what I once would have called "good" hair—but wasn't Mama "fair," her skin lighter-colored in summer than many of her "white" colleagues at work? And she was certainly "Negro-black." She had always made sure we knew our black history. Weren't there books about and by W. E. B. DuBois, Frederick Douglass, Phillis Wheatley, Paul Laurence Dunbar, Langston Hughes, and on and on right there on the bookshelf? Hadn't we heard over and over how her grandfather, Payton Flournoy Wade, had literally "slaved" to buy this property—which used to be ours all the way to the corner till some white county official decided it was too much land for a black man to own and took it upon himself to change the records? Little sister Monteith had to be coerced to know that brothers and sisters and other family members could be of widely differing hues and yet all be called "black."

Tom had struck a nerve at that late, night dinner when

he heatedly attacked the "one black drop" rule and its makers and guardians, including me. As he put it, "They're wrong! That's what's important! They're wrong . . . absolutely wrong!" Even as we argued, I knew, as did Tom, that color-coding people as black and white (or yellow or red or brown) could not be justified on biological or scientific grounds. The attempt to classify people as "black" because of that suspected "one black drop," although an absurd practice, was nevertheless a social reality for my parents and the generations before them. The idea of color-coded races had been reinforced by church, school and most other institutions in our society. We had been carefully told that in the United States of America "all men are created equal . . . with certain unalienable Rights" while, at the same time, being carefully indoctrinated that it was important to call ourselves by only one certain color, or "race," so that we could be treated in particular ways accorded to that color. Regardless of children's true physical coloring, or parents' misgivings at having to teach these things to their children, generation after generation was forced into one of the two molds: "white, Caucasian" or "black, Negro, colored." This wrong must have been especially obvious to thousands—millions—of little boys and girls of light skin colors, like my sister Monteith, as they were nurtured into "blackness" by the significant adults in their lives. Young though they were, they could recognize that their skin colors appeared to resemble "white" more than "black"; but still, they had to be taught that they were "black." At the same time, they were too young to understand the "why" of it all.

As it turned out, Tom and I decided to explore the implications of change, of looking at our child as the product of a union and no longer classifiable into either of the traditional "black" or "white" categories. We chose to describe people—not classify them. To provide for choice became our goal.

Three years later, our four-year-old daughter provided for us a very basic and simple lesson as related by her nursery school teacher. Monti was busy at play when a little "black" girl in her class scurried up to one child after another, pointing to each child and saying either "You're white" or "You're black." She approached Monti and blurted out, "You're black."

Monti, with no more than matter-of-factness, cast a quick glance at the little girl saying, "No, I'm not. I'm beautiful brown."

The little girl paused in momentary confusion, said no more and went on her way. Monti, untroubled and unruffled, continued her play.

We, as parents, soon after that Saturday night dinner confrontation, had agreed to refer to Monti as our beautiful brown daughter; "terrific tan" we told her. The above experience may illustrate how well she had internalized this concept already by age four. The simple, straightforward language of a child asks only that we look at what is, and then allow it to be.

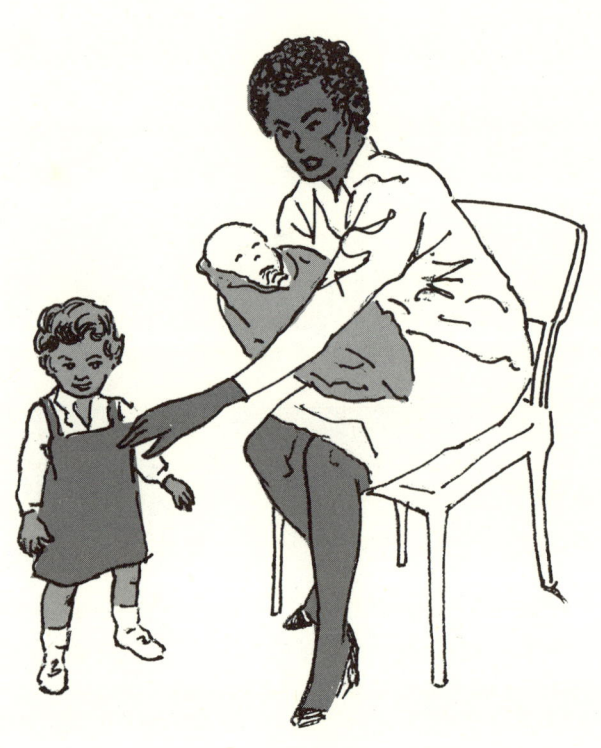

# 3

## *Are You from a Home*
### by Tom

"Soooo big!" said two-year-old Monti of her new baby brother Martin on the day we brought him home. Just seven weeks old, this fuzzy-haired, already smiling infant jerked and kicked his legs whenever he saw his "big" sister. He was "whiter-looking" than I, and his skin flushed bright pink whenever he became excited. My wife and I were told by one social worker: "Right now he's very fair; but don't worry, he'll 'brown up.' Children of mixed parents usually do in a year or two." Martin never did "brown up"! And that short, fuzzy hair, barely detectable in early infancy, grew into long, blond, shoulder-length curls. At sixteen months of age, Martin provided a sharp contrast to his newcomer brother's appearance.

Five-month-old Malcolm became our third child. His skin was silky looking and very dark brown, and his thick, kinky-curly, black hair was ready-made for the popular Afro style. Now five in number, our family seemed to capture a well-spaced, color chart of shades from eggshell-ivory to pumpernickel-brown.

People were soon to remind us that we did not fit conveniently the public's perception of either the "black" family or the "white" family. We grew accustomed to questions which often led us and others into awkward and embarrassing situations: "Are you together?" "Are these children with you?" "Do you work with children?" "Is this one yours?"

I recall vividly the first time I was asked the question, "Are you from a home?" Three-year-old Martin was on one side of me and two-year-old Malcolm on the other. We sat in one of those miniature, amusement park trains which are favorites of little people under six and welcome alternatives for many big people who no longer get their thrills by swirling in circles or nose diving on roller coaster tracks. The three of us, crammed into one seat, spanned the width of the narrow-gauge passenger car. The heavy-set engineer, who barely fit into the little locomotive, looked back patiently at the people boarding the small but long train. As I placed my arms around the wriggly and excited boys, the two elderly ladies seated directly in front of us smiled. I had assisted these senior citizens aboard.

"Are you from a home?" one lady asked.

While I am sure I expected that sooner or later I would be asked a question of this kind, I found myself unprepared to answer it. I hesitated; I even had half a mind not to answer it. Then, I said, "Oh yes, we have a home; we're a family."

"You certainly are a very kind man," said the other lady, nodding her head. "Is this a foster home?"

"No," I replied, not adding the most helpful information. I felt much like a child who reveals only a little of what he's thinking, expecting that the rest will be guessed. These two gray-haired, straight-shouldered, kind-faced ladies and I became snared in a trap of misunderstanding.

"Is the black one adopted?" she continued.

"Both my sons are adopted," I replied.

"Oh, that's nice," she said. "Do you have any real children of your own?"

I leaned back in my seat, looked to Martin, then to Malcolm, and said, pointedly, "These are my REAL children." The feeling of displeasure at being asked that question pounded in my shoulders, arms and stomach and, I am sure, my voice. The boys, their eyes and ears riveted to the maze of rides and the resounding yells of swirling, falling and topsy-turvy people, showed no interest in the suggestion that they might not be "real." In this instance, they were spared the hurt. As parents, we have learned to cry out in protest against this alienating notion that a child can be part of a family and yet not be "real." Familial bonds between parents and their adoptive children develop and grow much the same as do those between parents and children born to them. True and close relationships—"real" ones—are built through concern, caring and mutual respect, not simply through so-called blood ties. How many times does one hear "She's closer to me than my own sister" or "He helps me more than my own brother!"

The quiet that suffused the compact, open railway car was broken by the little engine's "Toot! Toot! Toot!" I remember the "Jack Frost" painted on the side of the locomotive as well as the chilly atmosphere which set upon our small passenger car. As we toured the park, there were no more smiles, no more nods and no nice words for the "kind" man who had taken two children from a "home" to the amusement park for a day.

These sorts of incidents are transitory; they hardly last longer than the train ride in the park. While the episodes themselves are short-lived, the afterthoughts, reflections or replays—what I should have said or what I could have said—linger on and are never quite complete. In these situations I have learned that a little patience and some straight answers and information can help to reduce rather than raise tensions. People are often inquisitive about things they see as new or different. Sometimes they ask questions out of curiosity as they prepare to be complimentary, sympathetic or approving. It's unfortunate when their questions give way to silent or open hostilities.

We grew to six in number when one-year-old Marquita

became a member of our family. We quickly reached seven as she was followed closely by three-year-old Meredith. By then, our older children had come to expect questions such as "Is this a nursery school outing?" or "Are you with the Jefferson School group?" On Sundays, the query was more likely to be "Is your Sunday School taking a trip today?" The children learned early in their lives that the issue really being addressed in these questions was the connection among us—being seen as individuals and yet unseen as a real family.

# 4

## *Seen, Yet Unseen*
### by Stanli

"Oh, I was looking right at it and couldn't see it" rings as a familiar phrase to grocery store clerks. At some time or other, most of us probably hunt for some item we want and overlook it. Careful second-searching doesn't always reveal it either, and we become frustrated as a result. Then, we may feel silly when we ask for help, and someone else quickly finds what we were seeking. Sometimes we poke around for a product and fail to recognize it because the packaging has changed. That familiar fruit juice, for example, which may have a newly designed label, or the occasionally purchased one that changes "overnight" and appears in a bottle or even a box instead of the traditional can, could lead a person to look directly at it but not "see" it.

People tend to have fixed associations, set ways of thinking that cause difficulty in perceiving change readily or in sensing something different with regard to the familiar. The juice name and the juice itself didn't change, but those trying to find the container experienced a problem in recognizing it. The same can happen when the so-called product is a family. Witness.

In the spring of 1979, only three months after three-year-old Meredith had joined our family, we prepared to take our first, long train trip. Excitement prevailed as the time arrived for the family excursion from Ohio to Texas via Amtrak. Tom had a convention in Dallas, and that was good enough reason for all of us to want to see this territory known to the children mostly through television and school. They were thrilled with the idea. As they put it, "We get to spend all day, all night and almost all day again on a train!" We had secured sleepers from Kansas City to Dallas; the anticipation of lying in berths, able to look out the window while envisioning a TV-type, Wild West, was almost too much for the children to bear.

Departure time arrived before nine o'clock on a Saturday morning. Only a half dozen or so people awaited the train in the downtown Dayton Amtrak Station. I boarded first. The children, clutching their activity bags, special toys and stuffed animal companions, stood spellbound before this huge, full-sized train which they could reach out and touch. Tom lifted the little ones and passed them to me and a porter who had stepped forward to help. The older three, ages five, six and eight, expressed their irritation at the notion of being lifted. For them, climbing up those high steps into the passenger car was part of the adventure.

"Come on, this way," I directed them to follow me once on board. The porter kept asking: "Is this one yours? . . . This one, too? . . . The little one here?" (Marquita had turned the wrong way.) The first car we entered had lots of passengers, but I remembered the porter's whisper when I thanked him, "Go back three cars, and there's plenty of room."

"Hold your things," I said. "We have to pass through another car. Look down the aisle and keep walking." The children were busy trying to look out the train windows and at the seated passengers. Despite my cautioning, they bumped their way through the crowded passenger car with hardly a glance to see what was in front of them. Sure enough, there were only seven or eight other passengers in the third car. I passed all of them, going to the seats nearest the far door. My arms were aching as I put down my paraphenalia—the two carry-on-bags, the heavy-duty, all-purpose, canvas purse and the combination snack-first-aid-diaper bag. "Okay, choose a seat. Anyone who wants a window may have one," I said.

"I'll sit here," said Monti, picking the window seat two rows behind me. "Marquita, you can sit on my lap." Giggling nervously, two-year-old Marquita, in my mind the spitting image of Monti at that same age, accepted. She pulled her bag and dolls onto the seat next to her big sister.

"Malcolm, sit with me . . . c'mon, Malcolm . . . please?" Pale, blond Martin cajoled his year-younger, but heavier, brown-skinned brother. "Ooooh-kay," was husky, frog-voiced Malcolm's answer. There was no tussling or complaining as they quickly dropped their things on the floor and went to the window. Malcolm kneeled on the seat while Martin leaned against the side of the car, arms propped on the window.

"You sit with me," Tom directed as he helped Meredith onto the seat next to the window opposite the boys. Meredith was visibly upset, ready for more tears. Traveling was especially hard for this little fellow. He was still so new to the family. Meredith's anxiety had begun the day before, on the first leg of the trip. We had driven to Nana's house in Dayton, about 230 miles from home. He kept asking, "Am I coming back?" In the last twenty-four hours he must have asked this question a hundred times. Martin assured him—as had all the children, with hugs and kisses—"Yes, Meredith, we all are. A family is not a house, it's people. You're gonna stay with us. Mom and Dad will take us all back to Shaker Heights when it's time."

Meredith escaped into sleep from nervous exhaustion almost as soon as he was in his seat, getting some sense of security by lying against Tom, his "new" dad. The train had begun to move and was picking up speed quickly. Squeals and shouts of "Look! Look!" permeated the area.

The children were preoccupied when the conductor appeared in the door closest to me. "TICKETS . . . tickeeeeets . . . cominthrupleesehavemready" is what I thought I heard. I reached into the zippered pocket of my purse where I had carefully counted and stashed them. He looked over his half-glasses at me as I opened the envelope.

"Seven of us," I said, beginning to gesture. "Two behind me, two behind them, two over there, and, of course, me with the tickets." I handed them to him. Since the other seats around us were vacant, I didn't look back to confirm places.

This gray-haired conductor of long-time, ticket-taking-on-trains experience peered in the direction of the seats I had indicated. He walked a few steps down the aisle to where Tom, his head reclined to face the window, was cuddling Meredith, now snoring loudly. Then, while looking from side to side, the trainman slowly backed up to where I was sitting. "Where are they?" he said in a puzzled tone. "I don't see them."

This puzzled me, and I leaned around the back of my seat to check—each person sat where I had described. I began to detect the problem. The "product" appeared to be a family, that is, an adult woman, an adult man with a child sleeping at his side, two more little boys and two little girls. But the "package" was not recognizable in its multishaded browns, tans and creamy-pinks.

"Oh, there they are," I said in a friendly fashion—but ready to burst into laughter. "They're all here."

Looking at the tickets he was holding and then at this assortment of people, he asked, "What is this? Two families traveling together?" The conductor was curious.

"No, just one," I stated.

"Hmmmm," was his only response as he looked at me, his eyebrows raised. He punched the tickets and handed them to me, saying in a throaty voice, "Here ya go. Have a nice trip!" He took two or three steps, stopped, and said in tones that sounded well practiced with children, "Kids, look out the window on this side (he pointed which way), and in about an hour you'll see buffaloes in a park. Have a good trip!" He moved quickly toward the other passengers at the far end of the car.

"Thanks!" I called, although I don't think he heard me.

"Life goes on," sighed sleepy-eyed Tom in soft tones, meant primarily for my ears. I could hardly stifle my laughter.

Initially the conductor had not been able "to see the forest for the trees." He had anticipated a family group traveling together, and he had been right. Because of his "mind set," fixed associations, in other words, about the way families should look, he saw a variety of individuals who did not fit his expectations; thus, he did not "see" our nontraditional family. We were seen, yet unseen.

# 5

## Smoke Clouds on a Desegregated Bus
### by Tom

The little Beckers had travel fever. One hot, muggy, August day, our family of seven squeezed into our little two-door Datsun B210 and headed for the downtown Cleveland Greyhound bus station. "Move over!" "Ouch!" "You're sitting on my leg!" shouted little voices from bodies pinned under travel bags. We were a one-car family at that time. If automobiles could have talked, our tiny, orange subcompact might have told tales about passenger life which would have stunned the largest of wagons and vans. Martin, our thin and wiry son, assigned the name "dinosaurs" to those larger vehicles; they looked so big to him as he constantly maneuvered for window space among the cramped, tangled arms and legs of his brothers and sisters. As a tot, Martin had admired those TV cartoon characters who rode dinosaurs.

Driving to the Greyhound station began the 230 mile trip to visit grandmother for a week. Traveling this distance on a public bus was a first for the children, and they were excited. Traffic was heavy in front of the bus terminal. Our best chance of reaching the bus on time was to double-park. So we did. That's part of big city life. We prepared—braced, I should say—for the unloading. Five or six people looked in amusement as the Datsun's doors were flung open; children bounced out quickly on the heels of the two adults. The fifth child, and the last to exit, jumped out with arms raised and body bowing, as does the last clown in the popular circus act where clown upon clown in seemingly endless succession step forth from a tiny car. Why shouldn't the children, in clownlike fashion, have fun after these jam-packed, though short, drives? On their own, as if planned, they did, with the last child out always seeking the most attention.

"Mom, I want you to come, too," said Martin, setting the stage for the farewell ritual.

Stanli quickly embraced her six-year-old son and smothered him with good-bye kisses. "I can't go this time, punkin. Mom has to stay home, watch the house and do some work."

I alone knew that, if anything, the coming too few days would be for my wife a mother's vacation at home.

"Dad, can I carry this bag?" asked Malcolm.

"Yes, son, . . ." Before I could get another word out, two-year-old Marquita tripped over one of the travel bags, fell to the concrete and burst into tears. What a sight: bags and suitcases scattered around the sidewalk side of the double-parked Datsun; petite, crying Marquita barely visible behind one of the suitcases; and I, wondering how everybody got into this small car in the first place. There are times when I stop what I'm doing and just stare in utter amazement, and I try to remember how I got into all of this. I even marvel that it's taking place. If I were to say something, it might be, "I quit!" I think the children sense this. Sometimes, the older children move quickly, almost as if to prevent such a declaration on my part. That happens when the risks to them involve the loss of anything from vacation trips and amusement park outings to ice cream, candy or other cherished juvenile delights.

Stanli was quick to rescue Marquita. "C'mon, children," she said. "I'll help Marquita with her things. You help Dad get the other suitcases and bags together." I knew that my dear wife had a lot to gain by getting us on the bus—specifically, the peace and quiet of a house temporarily rid of five very active children . . . and me! Quickly, the older children moved bag and baggage to the front of the bus station. Stanli enfolded one after the other in her arms for more hugs, kisses and good-byes. Finally, with one eye on the approaching police officer, I embraced and maneuvered Stanli to the driver's seat. A kiss, "Good-bye, I love you," and away she pulled without a traffic ticket. Engulfed by their activity bags, several dolls, stuffed animals, the shopping bag and gallon thermos jug, the children waved their final farewells.

Long accustomed to the stares of others, I tried not to notice the double takes of the people around. I remembered ten or twelve years ago when Stanli's seven-year-old sister, visiting us for the summer, asked, "Why are people staring at us?" In Washington, D.C., in 1967, an "interracial" couple with a cute, tan-skinned child tagging along evoked many stares and glares. At that time I had answered, "Because Stanli is so beautiful, and I'm so handsome." Now I was too busy to be witty. Herding five small children, ages eight, six, five, three and two, on a trip like this was challenge enough for me. The bus bound for Dayton would leave in fifteen minutes, with or without the stared-at, almost complete family of different colors.

The glares of some onlooking adults were not out of amusement. A very tall, brown-skinned man had stopped loading suitcases into his car trunk. He rested his crossed arms on top of the car. A surly, disturbed look set upon his face. Who knows what was stirring in this man's mind? Was his visible annoyance caused by this "black" woman who had chosen a "white" man over her "own kind"? Was he troubled by my actions and me, a "white" father, giving directions to two of my sons, both darker-skinned than he, the distressed onlooker? Distinctly, our family activities interested him.

A middle-aged "white" woman stood motionless next to her suitcases, staring in a kind of "Did you ever!" stupor. Truly, she must have thought, could that little, light-skinned, blond "punkin" be the son of this "black" woman, whose hugs and kisses fell naturally upon all these children?

Adult expressions—warm, chilling, friendly or hostile, or just plain observing—meant not one thing or another to the children as they entered the station and waited for my signal. "Gate 11, kids," I nodded to them, and they bounced forth. Skillfully weaving through the heavy adult traffic, the older children secured their positions in the line.

Straggling behind, two-year-old Marquita and three-year-old Meredith, their personal travel bags dragging across the crowded station floor, trudged their way through a sea of towering adults. They finally made it to the line only to be greeted by, "Don't cut ... Ohhhh ... you're cutting!" The two little ones had yet to learn the meaning of that charge, so they looked, puzzled, at their accusers—indeed, their own big brothers. "That's okay, go on," said a person in the line. "You can join them." The waiting passenger gently pushed the fledgling travelers toward their brothers and sister in the now extended line. I thank the Good Lord for people who have the sensitivity to give a child a friendly push—and a father a lift—in a crowded bus station on a hot, summer day. It does make the job easier.

Now in line and waiting before the departure gate, the children stood rather quietly, looking ahead, inching up, frequently on tip-toes. This calmness, I believe, was in anticipation of the excitement and wonderment yet to come. Beyond the gateway loomed the marvels of the loading platform, the steep steps into the bus and the castlelike, vantage ground of the high-set, Scenic Cruiser seats. They knew these things from having watched their grandmother arrive and depart on these very same buses.

Within moments they would press their noses to the windows to look down upon autos, people and seemingly even trees against which children look ever so small. Perhaps a few adults will capture a part of these same wonders, but all too soon most of us become void of the younger mind's imagination. Just as grownups don't explore for robbers' caves nor dig for hidden treasure, it also becomes clear to children that adults—most of them—no longer find magic in bus stations. Though these actors, adults and children, may share a common stage, there is, as a rule, little communication or interaction between them about these magical happenings.

Oh yes, the double takes continued in the waiting line. Some people don't believe what they see and have to turn to look again. Others want to watch. My wife and I have learned to follow the lead of our children; it just isn't fun to stare back at these people.

We took seats in the rear of the bus, close to the lavatory. Before leaving home, each child made a "bathroom check," but already two hours had elapsed. I did harbor high hopes for dry pants all the way on this trip, but this was not the only reason for choosing these seats. Our children, like most youngsters, are fascinated by strange bathrooms. When presented the opportunity, they are sure to make at least one exploratory visit to a newly discovered bathroom, whether the over-hygienized restaurant type or the grubby, locked, hard-to-open toilet rooms at gas stations. "I have to go, Mom" is often a ploy for the need to go and check the hot air, press-button hand dryers and the other equipment which are more intriguing than those of the home bathroom. None, however, is as fascinating as the cramped, closet-sized lavatories found on buses and passenger trains. Our little confidants inform us that the real reasons they "go" so often are "to try and see the water hit the road or tracks" and "to see if the water in the toilet bowl has come up yet."

Taking this into account, I positioned the children in

these rear seats in the hope that they would be less disruptive to the other passengers, knowing well how the children love to run, wiggle and bump through narrow aisles. What a range of amusement activities for youngsters—the bathroom equipment, the push-button overhead reading lights and the release knobs for reclining and raising seats. At least, we'd be somewhat out of the way of others by sitting in the back of the bus—or so I thought. I had just settled in my seat when a rugged, dark brown-skinned man in an open-neck sports shirt boarded the bus and approached the rear. Upon seeing the children and me, he was annoyed, I sensed. Concerned that our physical location in these rear seats was not an alienating factor, I guess I took a deep breath.

"I'll be damned!" he exclaimed gruffly for all to hear. "We used to have to fight to get to the front of the bus . . . (he paused for a few seconds) . . . and NOW (in a louder voice) we have to fight to get to the back of the bus!" This stout, square-faced, not-too-tall man stopped one seat in front of me. His deep, brown eyes scrutinized this mix of young passengers. Inquisitively, he scratched the back of his neck under his imposing, bushy Afro. Confined in the back of the bus, we were indeed vulnerable for an incident. "What the hell is this?" he said, again surveying the children. "The Brownies, Cub Scouts, or something?"

"No, we're a family," I replied without much of a delay and in as calm a voice as I could manage under these circumstances. I was scared. His look told me that I needed to say something or do something else. I pointed to Martin and to his seat partner Meredith with short, kinky, black hair and skin color as dark as the now confused, broadshouldered man still blocking the aisle. "This is Martin," I said. "He's six . . . and his brother, Meredith; he's three." I continued, with a friendly nod, hoping to conceal my belly-based butterflies. "Behind them are

Monti and Marquita." I motioned to my two pony-tailed, tan-skinned daughters, "Monti is eight, and Marquita is two." The man's tilted head and wrinkled brow, his obvious confusion, and his welcome inaction all suggested that I should keep talking. I placed my arm around Malcolm, seated with me, and gave him a firm hug—mostly for the security that I needed—and said, "This is Malcolm, my five-year-old son." I admit that for a moment it crossed my mind to say that Malcolm's namesake was Malcolm X, but I didn't. I was ready to try anything to escape this predicament.

What was I to do next? Nothing. It was Malcolm who helped us turn the corner that day. His eyes flashing the excitement of this great bus adventure, Malcolm looked up at the bold, sturdy figure standing before him and smilingly asked, "Are you going with us?" The stranger said nothing, but his lips now revealed a slight, supple break as he appeared to take stock of his five-year-old inquisitor.

Malcolm is the family extrovert. He has that winning smile and a manner of setting his head to one side which, more often than not, elicit smiles from others. His is an engaging personality, open and sincere, and often theatrical. Physically, he was then at five, as he still is, very muscular and strong. He was first in his beginner's class to jump into the water in chilly 65 degree weather when June swimming lessons began. Malcolm became the most likely to succeed in getting a piece of the Colonel's chicken from the pool lifeguards on their lunch break. Marquita and Meredith loved for him to play Incredible Hulk with them. Yes, he really is named after Malcolm X.

Malcolm and his older brother and sister looked at the stranger; they knew it was his turn to say something. The two little ones were wise to my preoccupation with this big person, and they had already tested the lavatory door several times and peeked at the toilet. Monti, leaning across the aisle toward me and pointing to them, said, "Dad, they're getting by with murder." She glanced uneasily at both the other man and me as she talked.

He looked at each of the children in turn, "Do you mean to tell me that all these are your kids?"

"Yes . . . yes, they are."

"All your kids? Your own kids?" repeated the unbelieving man.

I nodded with an affirming grin.

"Oh, man! You're telling me . . . today . . . the way things still are today . . . that this is a family!" exclaimed the man in a manner which made him appear to have the need to hear out his own words. His hardset expression seemed to mellow; his brow became somewhat relaxed. Always will I believe that this turn was due to the warm, inviting way in which Malcolm asked the man, "Are you going with us?"

The stranger knew that the older kids had tuned in to him. "You know, this here world ain't always been a very nice place for me to live in . . . yeah," he continued in a more subdued tone. "But today . . . right now, that is . . . you know, it's a hell of a lot nicer. A hell of a lot nicer because of you . . . right here." He pointed in a circular fashion to each child. "Yeah, because of what y'all doing right here."

Only then did I notice that we were not the only passengers captured by these words. Blocked in the aisle behind the man were two middle-aged women and a younger girl with a large, bulging, emblazoned bag draped about her shoulder. Several other seated passengers had noticeably shifted their positions, cocking their ears to hear what was being said behind them. Of course, the younger two Beckers were still too busy with the buttons and knobs—not to mention the lavatory door—to attend to this adult verbal interaction, imponderable to them anyway. Monti was right: the little ones had gotten by with "murder" while I was busy with the big man in the aisle. Malcolm, Martin and Monti were captivated by the words of this stranger; their eyes sparkled with excitement, too, with each "hell" and "damn" said. These are some of the words I think they play with when Dad and Mom aren't within earshot.

"AND," enunciated the once again very vocal gentleman for all to hear, "if there were more families like yours in this country, it would be a hell of a lot better place for me to live." Casting his eyes toward the front of the bus, he added, "And a hell of a lot better place for all of us to live in!"

The two women standing behind him moved toward the front of the bus to take seats, it appeared, to put some distance between them and the dominating aisle-orator. I really thought he was about to shout after them. Thankfully, he didn't.

"I want to shake your hand," he said, turning back to me. He placed his free hand warmly over the handshake, "Stay right where you are. I can smoke right here." He pointed to the first seat outside of the smoking section across the aisle from where I sat. Finally, he did take a seat, lighting the first of many cigarettes to come.

Only the young girl—a college student, I thought—with that large canvas bag on her shoulder moved past us to a seat behind ours. She nodded and smiled, noticeably at the children. There appeared to be a distinct sign of relief on her face, too, as she sat down and searched through her bag. Out came her cigarettes and a lighter. Within moments, a few puffs of smoke seemed to push her head relaxingly against the headrest.

Then it struck me. The children and I were taking up more than half of the eleven seats reserved for smoking. I understood, then, what the man had meant at first, about fighting for a seat in the rear of the bus. We had been challenged initially by a dedicated chain smoker, and I didn't realize until the closing seconds of this incident that smoking may have been foremost on the stranger's mind when he entered the bus.

No one else was stirring much, and I decided that we

would stay put rather than chance any further excitement. Very honestly, I do believe that a few passengers decided against smoking on this particular trip rather than risk being too close to whatever was going on.

The seats immediately in front of us had remained empty, not surprisingly, during this drama. No one else came on board to fill them. The bus driver, absent during most of this episode, finally took his seat, and we were on our way within minutes.

Smoke clouds on a desegregated bus . . . that's what I thought as I breathed another sigh of relief and settled back in my seat. I did tell this man my name, and I asked him his. I don't know that he even told me. I looked at him sitting diagonally across the aisle in front of me, lighting a new cigarette against the old. The smoke seemed to fade gently in upward movements. The complexity of heavy Chester Avenue traffic contrasted sharply with the now slow tempo of passenger life aboard the bus.

We had been on the interstate highway hardly ten minutes when six-year-old Martin popped the question I've learned to expect during the first half hour of any trip. "Dad, may we eat now?"

"Dad, I have to go to the toilet first," said another voice.

"Me, too," said another.

I motioned one to the lavatory. I reached for the brown bag packed with peanut butter and jelly sandwiches, apples, cookies and cups. I pushed the thermos of apple juice closer with my foot. After all, for the children, much of the success of this great bus adventure depended on what came now.

# 6

## *Mirror Images*
### by Stanli

The children were eager to tell me about the man on the bus.

"Mom, he thought we were the Cub Scouts or Brownies or something," said Martin.

"The Brownies? That certainly was silly, Martin. I know Brownies are girls. Monti was a Brownie," I said playfully. "And the Cub Scouts are boys!"

"I know that, Mom!" said future Cub Scout Martin.

"Yeah, we know, Mom! We know that!" chimed in other little voices.

"Dad told him we were a family," said one.

"He was nice then," said another.

"He told us the world was better now," said Martin proudly.

"Better?" I raised my eyebrows in contrived curiosity. "Better? Why would it be better?"

"Because of us, Mom! Because of us! Yeah! Yeah, Mom!" cried out the children amidst the giggles now filling the room. They knew I was having fun with them as we joined in laughter. Their encounter with the man on the bus had left them with the most positive afterthoughts. The stranger on the bus had truly been "out front" with the children.

Seldom are unfamiliar people open and frank and

praising of the family. Rarely does anyone in public acknowledge to the children that they are doing something that may be out of the ordinary, difficult and worthwhile. Martin, in particular, was to retell this story to others, including some of his friends and teachers. He has been challenged by his buddies—both "black" and "white"—to explain his "crazy" family. This incident gave him ammunition, supplied by an outsider, to point out the "good things," as Martin put it, about his different family. Sometimes his listeners didn't understand—or didn't want to understand—this message which Martin has come to treasure.

How and when children like Martin, his brothers and his sisters become aware of either hostilities toward or support and plaudits for their "interracial" family is not really clear. Tom and I believe that first impressions occur very early in their lives. Martin says he does not remember the man in the supermarket who once scolded his sister Monti, but the incident remains indelibly fixed in my memory.

A child with brown eyes, blond hair, skin coloration of tan, pink and creamy-white, just like the skin colors of most "white" people, will be just that—"white"—to the person passing by. So it was for Martin when he sat in the supermarket shopping cart at age one.

"You leave him alone!" snorted the past-middle-age man, hair graying, pointing and shaking his index finger at Monti.

Almost four, pigtails bobbing, my pretty, beige-skinned daughter stared at the meddling man who looked very much like her "white" grandfather. She held two packages of meat she had just taken from her baby brother who was in the grocery cart. As Monti put them back in the meat case, Martin leaned over the shopping cart and grabbed another package. "Give it to me, Martin!" yelled Monti, as she pulled on the roast.

"Don't bother that baby," grumbled the man. Monti

turned to glare at him. He didn't know that her mother had told her to watch her little brother.

"I can reprimand my own children . . . if they need it!" said a new voice to the man. I had been selecting meat from a counter a few feet away.

"This little girl is bothering him," reported the man, pointing first at Monti, then at Martin.

"I can take care of my own children," I retorted in a voice getting louder with each word.

The man was very protective of this little, blond, "white-looking" boy whom he saw as being harassed by the bigger, little "black" girl. "I don't know where his mother is," he blurted out in tones approaching anger and annoyance, "but the girl is bothering this baby!" He was looking for still another child as he spoke since this "black" woman, obviously the little girl's mother, had said she could take care of her children.

Using a much louder but distinctly civil voice, causing other shoppers to move toward us and stare, I responded, "THESE ARE BOTH MY CHILDREN, AND THIS IS NOT YOUR BUSINESS!"

The man, now quite flustered, looked from Martin to Monti to me as he backed away. This was too confusing for him. A "black" woman was claiming this "white" baby as her child. Muttering to himself, the man moved into the gathering crowd, inching his way down the aisle, and disappeared from our view. Had this man been more discerning initially, he might have noted that Monti did call Martin by name, indicating some kind of relationship. But such is the myopic vision of prejudice: one sees or hears only what one wants to see or hear.

A couple of shoppers who saw me with the children in the store regularly came to ask what had happened. The others went back to their groceries, seeing that the excitement had ended. I was convinced that my technique of handling this confrontation had worked. The method of talking loudly to attract and gather people—possible witnesses, if necessary—was my way of protecting my children and myself. I believe that the larger the observing group, the greater the probability that one person present will tell the truth, whatever his or her motive. Should something serious ever happen to me or the children in a public setting, lots of people would see it. Surely, at least one would step in to help me or be willing to substantiate whatever I reported to have happened.

I began talking to the children, in particular to Martin. "It's Mommy's job to fill the cart with meat." I took a much needed, deep breath now that the crowd had dispersed, hugged Martin, saying again, "That's Mommy's job." I put one arm around Monti, thanked her, and pushed the cart down the aisle with my free hand, as mothers learn to do.

Martin was recognized as "white" for the moment. His curly, bright, yellow hair and light-colored skin gave him a mirror image of "whiteness," assumed by the interfering man to be the same as his own. A safe guess would be that this man, like so many of us, was taught from his earliest years to fit "blacks" into one mental box and "whites" into another. This is but one of the fallacies adults fall back upon to sustain them in a complex world beset by mistrust and uncertainty; it is, I have come to believe, the "most dangerous myth" our society teaches.

# 7

## *Reductio Ad Absurdum*
### by Stanli

"Blacks are different. Let's face it; we all know it. Forcing them and us together isn't going to work." The speaker went on to address the issue of integration before his listeners, all of whom he assumed where "white." But even as he spoke, the speaker was unaware that the small, mirror-image "white" group before him was not "pure white." Not more than ten feet from him sat a person who, although "white-looking," was the product of a "black-white" marriage.

Assumptions about others who seem to be "white," based on casual observations of skin colors, are made by many "white" people; to them, a person who appears to be "white" should be "white"—and that means "pure white." The above speaker typifies those "whites" who may not be cognizant of light-skinned, "white-looking" people who have that "one black drop" in their biological composition. Too many Americans simply do not want to know about those mirror-image whites who do not reflect their mixed heritage and origins. Through specious reasoning, these Americans allow themselves to believe that an individual is either "pure white" or not; they engage in a head-in-the-sand type denial of what centuries of "interracial" unions have begotten. This is what Nobel Prize winner Gunner Myrdal considered fundamental to an understanding of skin color prejudice in this nation. In his classic study *An American Dilemma: the Negro Problem and Modern Democracy*, Myrdal said: "the concern for 'race purity' is basic in the whole issue; the primary and essential command is to prevent amalgamation; the whites are determined to utilize every means to this end."[4] And throughout the history of our nation, seemingly every means has been used to prevent amalgamation, that is, so-called race-mixing between "blacks" and "whites." Myrdal allowed no room for doubt in pointing out that the denial of social equality to "blacks" was designed particularly to prevent intermarriage.

Many obstacles to social equality in housing, education, religion, politics and the judicial system have fallen since Myrdal published his two-volume report in 1944. However, history appears to have proven the Swedish scholar Myrdal right in respect to the emphasis he placed upon "white" resistance to racial intermarriage. Statutory laws forbidding intermarriage between "blacks" and "whites" were not declared unconstitutional by the Supreme Court until 1967. This ruling took place thirteen years after the Court's historic decision prohibiting segregation in the public schools. During these thirteen years, this highest court of the land had three opportunities to review and to rule on the constitutionality of these antimiscegenation statutes. It did not. Scholars, other than Myrdal, have suggested that this delay was by design—that the issue of interracial marriage before the Supreme Court was, indeed, a "bombshell," moreso even than that of school desegregation.[5]

Despite the purging of many laws to rid the land of legalized "racial" discrimination, it has been clear, nevertheless, that many community, business and government leaders seem bent on attempting to provide continued protection for the "white" masses, those belonging to the majority-skin-color culture. This is not to deny that within the American majority-skin-color culture there are notable subcultures which again and again divide people on more particular matters, but the basic expectations remain the same. That majority of Americans who are thought to be "pure white" secure freedoms, liberties and favors which are granted to minorities only by degrees and measures, affecting most facets of life such as working, worshiping, housing, schooling, convalescing, retiring, swimming, dancing, golfing and so on.

Those of the majority culture may be unaware of the securities inherent in the "white" majority way; they may have given little or no thought to the matter; they may not be privy to lifestyles which are based on secrecy and fear. I could cite examples of people who "work white and live black." In other words, they go to their jobs and allow themselves to be perceived as "white" in the workaday world. These mirror-image whites know that their jobs and financial security would be threatened if it were known that their parents, siblings or mates would be acknowledged as "black."

A friend related the circumstances of his elderly, great-uncle who is well situated in a lovely nursing home in a western suburb of Cleveland. "Some of us in the family can't visit him except by phone," the grandnephew reported, "because he looks white, and if any of us 'darkies' went to see Uncle, he would soon be evicted. He would have never been accepted there if they had known he is black."

Estimates of the number of "whites" who have some "black" ancestry range from the hundreds of thousands to numbers over twenty-five million. There may be anywhere from several thousand or so to tens of thousands annually who change the way they publicly identify themselves from "black" to "white."[6] On the other hand, some who could live in the "white" majority culture have chosen deliberately to be called "black" or "Negro."

One such person was the late, distinguished, American Negro leader Walter White, who was Executive Secretary of the National Association for the Advancement of Colored People during the very depressed and intensely segregated years of the 1930s and 1940s. He was a dominant and influential representative of "black" people for better than three decades. Dressed in the work clothes of the hometown southern "white," the courageous Walter White —veiled by his light skin, blond hair and blue eyes—entered "white" communities many times to investigate and report lynchings, mutilations and other atrocities against Negroes. He did so at great risk to his own person, and he barely escaped the hands of "white" mobs and lynchers during some of these dangerous ventures.

In 1949, the well-known Walter White was beset by controversy when his wife of 27 years obtained a divorce, shortly after which he married a woman friend of twenty years; she, Poppy Cannon, was a "white" woman. In her book *A Gentle Knight: My Husband, Walter White*,[7] Poppy Cannon wrote about the years they spent together, first as friends and then as husband and wife until his death in 1955. They traveled widely throughout the world in the months following their marriage, which had received international news coverage. In more than one foreign city, the "interracial" couple encountered some confusion about their racial identities. As Poppy Cannon put it: ". . . they [foreigners] jumped to the conclusion that I, being many shades more brunette than Walter, must be the colored partner."[8]

At the time Walter White's autobiography *A Man Called White*[9] went to press in 1948, he estimated that every year approximately 12,000 light-skinned Negroes "passed" into the white population. Walter White recognized that the notion of separate and distinct races could not be justified on scientific or biological grounds. He wrote: ". . . the root of my anger and my frequent deep discouragement . . . is founded on one of the most absurd fallacies in all thought—the belief that there is a basic difference between a Negro and a white man."[10]

The first lines of his autobiography read: "I am a Negro. My skin is white, my eyes are blue, my hair is blond."[11] Walter White was a Negro in mind and heart—not by the accident of skin color. Though he was accepted by both "blacks" and "whites" as a Negro, not one of the so-called physical traits of "blackness" was visible upon him. "Walter White represented, in my opinion, the supreme *reductio ad absurdum* [Latin, a reduction to the absurd] of any argument about race," wrote Poppy Cannon. "Looking at him made the whole matter take on the aspect of a huge joke . . . often it has been a grim joke!"[12]

The late John Hope, another outstanding Negro leader with whom our children have become familiar, was, like Walter White, a "white" man from all outward appearances. Hardly a family discussion on racial awareness or skin color passes without the book *The Story of John Hope*[13] being held by some little hands. This biography of a courageous, American educator is a family favorite, unusual because so often it has been the object of attention of the younger children before they learned to read. They reach for the book because of the hardback cover equally divided in contrasting solid black and solid white. When I place my arm against the black portion of the front cover, usually someone says gleefully, "See, Mom's skin is brown, not black!" Delightedly, the children will continue this skin-to-book matching in that childlike, ritualistic manner which typically claims all eyes and ears present: "Dad's pink, not white [sometimes tan, sometimes yellow]" or "That's black," as a tiny finger points to the book cover, "and my arm is dark brown! Right, Mom?" Occasionally, a very serious voice can be heard uttering, "Nobody here is really black or white."

*The Story of John Hope* was a gift to us some years ago from Dr. and Mrs. Edward Hope, whom we have come to know as very special, compassionate people and close friends. By good fortune, we became acquainted with Edward and Louise Hope not knowing in advance that we already shared some relationships. Tom first met Mrs. Hope through mutual interests they shared as professional educators. Neither of them at that time knew that the Hopes' grandchildren had become playmates with our children through a neighborhood play group. Nor did we connect Mrs. Hope with her married daughter, whom I had met through the children's activities. Moreover, unbeknownst to me, my dentist was the Hopes' son-in-law. One day, all these relationships were discovered. Shortly thereafter, we met Edward, the first born of the late John Hope. Our contacts, very limited up to this point, were soon to increase dramatically.

A not-to-be-forgotten evening it was, that first time Dr. and Mrs. Hope invited us to dine with them in their elegant condominium, only a short walk from historic Shaker Square in Cleveland. Tom and I stood before the directory in the glass-enclosed vestibule in a state of quiet anticipation. My finger moved down the list of names to Hope. "Hope," said Tom. "We must ask Dr. Hope to tell us about his father tonight." Tom and I knew of John Hope, but neither of us were yet aware of the influences this distinguished American, deceased by over forty years, was to have upon our lives. I picked up the intercom-telephone and pressed the button next to the Hopes' nameplate.

Our conversation was warm from the onset. We talked of the children and grandchildren, of how our families became acquainted, and of some curiously common experiences—the Hopes were sometimes perceived as an "interracial" pair. As we savored the tender cornish hens and flavorful wild rice before us, so did we relish the stories and experiences of the Hope family being recounted by our gracious and amiable hosts. At one point, Louise urged Ed, as he preferred to be called, to tell us of his early childhood experiences at Morehouse College. He was the elder son of John Hope, who served as president of Morehouse College during the turbulent years of racial hostility in the early 1900s. Ed could tell us now, with the wisdom of hindsight, why his father told him to be "an awfully good engineer" if he aspired to be one at all. He recalled for us the night terror of the Ku Klux Klan and how his father's presidency had begun under the shadow of the 1906 Atlanta race riots.

Ed took time to speak in reverent, affectionate tones of his father's contributions to American life. His father dedicated his lifetime to the struggle of "giving Negroes," as Ed phrased it, "the widest opportunities for education in the tradition of the liberal arts." He spoke of his father's difficult and delicate mission among Negro soldiers in France during World War I. I suppose we could have sat there the better part of the night listening to Ed.

" Who will have coffee?" asked Louise, making mental notes of the responses.

"Well, while Louise is tending to that, let me do something," interjected Ed. He stood up, walked to the buffet, picked up a book, and returned to his seat. He handed the book to Tom, saying, "This is the story of my father's life—a beautifully written account by Ridgely Torrence. I think it may be of interest to you and Stanli."

Over the next few weeks, Tom and I were to spend hours and hours reading, rereading and reflecting upon this biography of John Hope, in particular, how he had blended his affection for his Scottish background with his dominant love for his dark-skinned mother and "her people." Ed had given us more than a book.

John Hope was born in Augusta, Georgia, on June 2, 1868, of a well-to-do white Scot immigrant father and the daughter of a freed slave. John's parents lived in so-called "open alliance" as husband and wife even though the laws of Georgia did not recognize a legal marriage between a "white" man and a "colored" woman. They had been legally married in South Carolina. John appeared to be, as does our son Martin, a "white" child. Later, in John's college years, he made the choice to identify with his Negro mother and "her people," though his skin coloration was the same as that of the American majority—so-called white. It was a decision he made on the afternoon before his commencement at Brown University; John Hope turned his back on an alluring career in journalism in the North and returned South to become a teacher. "He rejected," said his son, Ed, in one of our many subsequent conversations, "the financial and psychological security of the white world; yet, he was to gain peace of mind by following his heart . . . it pulled him into the fold of his mother's people." John Hope's decision closed to him the guarantees and expectations presumed by members of the majority-skin-color culture as inherent in American life.

Despite his untimely death in 1936, John Hope lived to see some of his dreams become realities as he planned for and then put into operation the new Atlanta University, becoming its first president. "He made Atlanta University!" said Ed, during one of our many discussions on *The Story of John Hope*. "That was his brainchild," he continued, reminiscing on the glories of his father's achievements. Speaking persuasively, yet unpretentiously, about his father's accomplishments, Dr. Edward Hope may well have been at that moment the speaking likeness of his father, I thought. A trenchant conversant, Ed's blue-grey eyes flashed, albeit shyly, maybe humbly, with that same "patent honesty of purpose," which W. E. B. DuBois wrote was so characteristic of his father.[14]

W. E. B. DuBois and John Hope were contemporaries. On August 18, 1906, they stood together among a hundred people on a field before the reconstructed engine house where John Brown had made his last stand. "There was majesty in the scene, and there was majesty in the spirit of the pilgrims and in their cause," wrote Torrence. "Their cause was to find justice in their native land . . . , they sang the 'Battle Hymn of the Republic.' They were the members of the Niagara Movement."[15]

John Hope showed great courage in attending this Niagara Movement conference at Harpers Ferry, West Virginia. He was then president of Atlanta Baptist College, and he was the only person of his academic rank who ventured to be present at that historic meeting. "At that time, it [the Niagara Movement] was the most radical activity of the race, in direct opposition to the theories best supported by financial supply. For a newly-appointed head of a college wholly dependent on outside help, his course was precarious and even dangerous."[16]

"The death of John Hope removed an unusual figure from American life," wrote DuBois in the *Pittsburgh Courier*, March 28, 1936. He eulogized John Hope as one guided by "fine simplicity, . . . unselfish motives, and . . . delicate, almost painful fear of injustice," and as one who "was at once white and glad to be black."[17]

"I think what DuBois meant when he said Father was 'at once white and glad to be black,'" said Ed in one of our talks, "was that Father was white, because there were no so-called Negroid features. His nose was long . . . mine's stubby . . . see . . . his nose was longer than yours," as he pointed to Tom's nose, "and narrower. His eyes weren't just blue; they were blue-blue! I can remember other Morehouse students, having been called on the carpet, talking about how Father could look with those steely blue eyes . . . right into them." Ed paused momentarily before adding, "He would have been the perfect type to go over on the other side of the color line." Very deliberately, he continued, "Let me introduce this. Somewhere in the family somebody did not make the same choice as Father . . . he knew the person . . . and they maintained communication until Father died."

John Hope could have been, by his choice, a "white" American. That was not the path he chose. Regardless, he repeatedly had to disclose to others during his many travels in this country and throughout the world that he was not "white." "I'm a colored man," he would say. He was always ready and very determined to make known his chosen identity.

Tom and I strive to develop in our children an understanding of why men like Walter White and John Hope, in their times, chose to be "Negro," "colored" or "black" and not "white." But the very fact that Walter White and John Hope could have made a choice, just as many mirror-image whites can still do today, shows also how ridiculous is the concept of "race."

# 8

## *Music Has a Color Line, Too*

### by Martin

I look "white" to most other kids—adults, too! When I tell people I'm not "white," they often look surprised. Then, when I tell them I'm not "black" either, they become very confused.

Once I was walking to a friend's house with my "box" blasting away on WJMO. That's a local "black" radio station. I was about half a block away from my friend's house when this "black" guy about fifteen or sixteen years old stopped me and asked, "Hey, what's a white boy like you doing listening to black music?"

I was really scared. I was only nine and had just gotten my "box" for my birthday. I mean, look at the way older kids steal and even rob things from younger ones. My "box" is really cool, and I love it! It's over a foot long and almost a foot high with AM/FM stereo, radio and cassette recorder, timer and everything. I wasn't quick enough to run. I just stood in front of him with my mouth wide open. I didn't know what to do, so I didn't do anything.

"Don't you hear, boy?" he said. "What you listening to black music for?"

Dad and Mom always taught us kids to speak to the facts and move on. So I said, "I'm biracial. That's why I listen to black music. I can listen to white music, too." My voice was really squeaky. I started to back away, toward my friend's house.

The kid looked at me strangely and yelled, "What the ____ is biracial?"

"That's when you're part black and part white and really integrated," I said, walking faster. "I gotta go. My friend's waiting for me in that brick house there." I lied about the brick house, but it was closer to me than my friend's house. The boy didn't chase me. He just stared at me and shook his head. Then he turned around and walked away. I took a deep breath, kept walking backwards, and hugged my "box."

# 9

## *Race-Thinking*
### by Stanli

To believe that "white" people listen only to "white" music and "black" people listen only to "black" music is to succumb to "race-thinking." Jacques Barzun coined the term "race-thinking" in his 1937 book *Race: a Study in Modern Superstition*, and he defined it as the tendency "to think of human groups without the vivid sense that groups consist of individuals and that individuals display the full range of human differences."[18]

"Race-thinking" can affect basic daily activities and decisions. A telephone conversation I had with a restaurant hostess illustrates this:

| | |
|---|---|
| Stanli: | I want to arrange for a luncheon on September 10th for 20 to 30 people, and I'd like to know your menu selections. |
| Hostess: | Well, we could put you in one of the parlors. Let's see, for that number . . . let me get the menu. Would $5.95 be okay? |
| Stanli: | Yes, we'll start there. |
| Hostess: | Hmmm, salads. We have tossed, fruit, jello, cottage cheese, cucumber . . . |
| Stanli: | Just a moment, please. You're going too fast while I'm writing. |
| Hostess: | Okay. You're black, right? (short pause with no response from Stanli) You know we like tossed salads, right? |
| Stanli: | Could you explain that, please? |

| | |
|---|---|
| Hostess: | Well, you're black, right? (no pause) And I'm black, and we like tossed salads, right? |
| Stanli: | Well, I do like tossed salads, but how do you know this? |
| Hostess: | C'mon. We all know that black people like tossed salads, greens and stuff like that, right? |
| Stanli: | Could you give me the other menu selections, please? |

Whether because of voice timbre or some "telltale" remark on my part, the hostess made a judgment about my identity. I was rather surprised! More than not, my telephone identity, I am told, is that of a "white" person speaking. A professional person, upon meeting my husband for the first time on business related to school integration, stared at him for a moment and said, "I knew you were white. I talked to your wife on the telephone. I can always tell a white voice." How surprised that man was to be introduced to Tom's graham cracker color-skinned wife with a full, bushy Afro later that evening. Some of my own business acquaintances, having talked to me on the phone before meeting me in person, have remarked, each in his or her own way—and identifying himself or herself as black—"I'm really surprised! I didn't know you were a 'sister.' I thought you were white, especially with a name like yours and the way you sound on the phone."

"Race-thinking" calls for one to be in accord with categorical generalizations: "Blacks speak a black dialect." "Whites listen to white music." "Blacks prefer tossed salads." At this writing, the only difference we've detected among our children concerning tossed salads is in the amount each child serves, due no doubt to parental policy: "Serve yourself only what you can eat and clean your plate, that is, if you want dessert." The children listen to the music they like—both "black" and "white," even classical, on occasions. And we parents don't teach "white" or "black" English!

The children are encouraged to discuss their individual tastes and preferences, and they learn to accept obvious physical differences among themselves and others without stamping these traits as "black" or "white." It is amusing, from time to time, that a child with straight hair envies one using a pick, a comb used primarily for Afro hairstyles. Martin was six when he got tired of "just plain ol' hair," as he put it.

A loud "Ouch!" hastened me to the scene of steel spikes being pushed too hard against a tender scalp. There stood Martin on a footstool before the mirror in the small, first-floor bathroom plowing a big pick-type comb through his blond, straight hair having barely a hint of a curl. "Ah, ha, ha, ha!" came the deep, rumbling laughter from five-year-old Malcolm, standing on his tiptoes beside Martin and looking into the mirror also. "Martin, you look funny!" Martin, his feelings hurt, as was his head, turned his tear-filled eyes to me, "It's not funny, Mommy. I want to use the Afro comb, too. I want my hair to be big like Malcolm's."

Hugging sad, annoyed Martin, I thought it was time for a quick family conference. I called out, "Everybody come here for a minute, please?" Malcolm tried to stop laughing as he joined Monti and Tom at the breakfast table. Martin sat on my lap, gnawing on his fingernails.

"You know, we've probably talked hundreds of times about how our family is different, how each of us looks different from one another," I began. "Let's talk about hair for a minute. Look at Dad's hair. It's brown with gray in it. Most of it is straight, but he has some waves and a few curls on top; and he had some curls in the back when he wore it longer, remember? Now look at mine. Remember when I had those chemicals in it to make it straight? I had to put rollers in it to make it curly. Now I'm wearing a short 'natural', and I just wash it, oil it, and comb it."

Monti interrupted, "Mom, remember when you had a

great, big Afro, and you put curlers in it at night to keep it gigantic?" Everyone nodded, remembering.

"Yes, that was part of keeping it groomed then, Monti," I replied. "What about your hair, Monti?"

"Well, mine is brown and straight at the bottom (pointing to her roots) and curly at the ends. Sometimes I put rollers in it after I wash it to make it have nice curls on the ends when I wear it down. Or, I can wear it in pigtails with barrettes so it won't come loose. Sometimes I wish my hair were straight, but mostly I like it."

Monti, at age eight, had obviously thought about her hair, hanging well below her shoulders.

"Malcolm, you have a beautiful Afro," Tom said. "Mom keeps it nicely cut."

"I know it," said Malcolm, patting his round, thick, curly hair. "Martin's hair is flat. That's why my pick hurts his head. The pick hurts my hair when I have to get the tangles out, but it doesn't stick my head like it does Martin's." Then Malcolm looked at Martin and said affectionately, "I like your hair, Martin. Anyway, you're the only one with yellow hair, and it's pretty."

Martin had listened quietly and thoughtfully through yet another family conference. He seemed to feel better as he said, "Remember when I was a baby and had those curls on my shoulders? That's what I want—long hair, a ponytail like . . . ." (He named a male neighbor-friend, high-school student.)

"Aw, Martin," said Monti, as the family members started to move away from the table, returning to whatever they had been doing. Martin was okay now and back to playing. Another small crisis had passed.

As parents, we capitalize on practically every opportunity to focus the children's attention on the wide range of individual differences which exist among people. To ignore individual differences is to court that kind of "race-thinking" which leads one to believe that "blacks" prefer tossed salads. Carried to its extreme, "race-thinking" leads one group of people to believe itself superior to another in such traits as intelligence, ambition, industriousness and even morality.

J. A. Rogers, in his novel *From "Superman" to Man*,[19] unleashes a penetrating attack upon these ill-founded notions. It is a book that one day I will ask my children to read. The plot centers on a well-educated and world-traveled Negro porter Dixon who engages a condescending U.S. Senator from Oklahoma in discussion on the issue of racial superiority. The senator, a passenger on Dixon's train, personifies that extreme racial ideology of America which depicts Negroes as inferior beings. His stories and jokes about "darkies," "coons," "watermelon feasts" and "chicken stealing" mark him as a real, practical prototype of the "Sambo" creators of the 1920s, 1930s and 1940s. During this period of United States history, the "Sambo" image makers concocted a stereotyped black person who was not supposed to be compatible in any way, shape or form with the "pure white" American. This "Sambo-Negro," even featured in the movies, had big, bulging eyes, hair standing on end, lips protruding; his childlike fear of ghosts caused him to shudder and cry, "Lawd, ha' mussy! De daid am riz!"; he was an easygoing, foot shuffling, slack-jawed comedian, melodizing "Eaney Meany Miney Mo!" Boys and girls were to read *Little Black Sambo*, while adults were to enjoy jokes about happy, carefree colored "boys" who sat around singing or shooting craps.

Dixon confronts the senator in the manner of a skilled, courteous debater, countering and refuting each of the senator's prejudiced views. Through the patient and polished deliberations of the Yale-educated porter, J. A. Rogers provides the reader with an astounding array of facts drawn from anthropology, science and history to illustrate that "color prejudice is only the result of certain ignorant teachings."[20]

Another of Roger's books, *100 Amazing Facts about*

*the Negro with Complete Proof*,[21] presents a multitude of enlightening facts which expose many of the misconceptions and outright lies about "blacks" which have been heaped upon Americans for centuries. Perhaps of greater importance are those works by Rogers, *Nature Knows No Color-Line* and *Sex and Race* (3 volumes),[22] documenting the vast amount of worldwide "race-mixing" which has taken place from the earliest days of Greece and Rome to twentieth-century America. His extensive research led him to believe "that it is possible for anyone, no matter who, to have had among tens of thousands of his ancestors at least one Negro."[23] That Americans continue to draw sharp lines between "black" and "white" is a social reality; that this practice is also the end result of decades of "ignorant teachings" is unquestionably the truth! Rogers wrote: "the points of unlikeness between so-called races are nothing compared with those in which they are alike."[24]

# 10

## *Where's Your Mommy*
### by Meredith

I like to go to the grocery store with Dad. I always try to be good. But it's soooo hard. One time I didn't get a treat because I poked a hole in the top of a cake. Dad didn't want to buy the cake. The store lady got angry! Dad got angry! He made me wait by the door. I watched him check out. I felt sad, and I cried. I was only five years old.

The next time Dad took me to the store, he let me push the shopping cart. He said, "Keep your hands on the cart, and don't touch the food!" We started to shop. Dad stopped and looked at me when we got to the fruit. I thought he was going to say, "Don't bump the cart on my heels." He didn't. He did say, "Don't punch the peaches!"

"Ooookay," I said.

We moved some more. I stopped to look at the grapes. Dad turned around. He pointed and said, "Don't touch the grapes!"

"Ooookay!" I said. I was being good, and I put both hands on the cart.

The next thing Dad told me not to bother was the big barrel of peanuts we passed. That was really hard. I love peanuts.

Dad stopped at the lettuce. He always feels it. I love to touch and feel food, too. And I love to eat. I looked back at the peanuts. Dad saw me and said, "Don't go near the peanuts!"

A dark brown-skinned lady, the same color as I am, came up to me and bent down. She looked right at me and whispered, "Little boy, where's your mommy?"

"She's at work," I told her.

"Well, honey, who are you with?" she asked me. I didn't answer, but I looked at her real hard. At Safety Town we learned not to talk to strangers.

"Who brought you into the store, sweetie?" she said to me.

"My dad," I said.

"Oh, good," she said. "You hurry up and go find him, and don't pay attention to what that white man says."

I didn't know what white man she was talking about. I stared at her with my hard look again. I went and held Dad's hand. Then, I wondered if she meant my dad. I gave her another hard look.

Dad put the lettuce in the cart. He knew that I wanted to hold his hand, so he pushed the cart. The lady stared at Dad and me as we moved down the aisle. I stared back . . . real, real hard.

Dad winked and smiled at me at the check-out counter. He bought me a treat, a big lollipop. He told me I was good, too!

# 11

## *The White Grandmother*
by Tom

Experiencing a kind of invisibility, being seen yet unseen, is not limited to the immediate "interracial" family. Members of the extended family also assume new roles in which they essentially become "invisible" to those who are unaware of the "interracial" family ties.

My mother Mary Kae, the children's "white" grandmother, usually accompanies us in the summer to a beach resort for several days of family vacationing. Nana, as the children fondly call her, loves to walk the sandy beach in the morning and bathe in the afternoon sun. She takes pleasure in renting surf rafts for her grandchildren, watching them battle the breaking waves . . . and sometimes each other.

One afternoon as Nana relaxed on the beach some distance from where the children were splashing and rolling on their rafts, a man of her own generation strolled by and began a conversation with her. Talkative and preoccupied with the aches and pains which had brought him to the resort and the nearby health clinic, this senior citizen was ready to disclose his complete medical history to Nana. She politely focused her comments on the beautiful beach, tropical weather, and carefree water play of both young and old. The man, yielding to her pleasure, turned his attention to vacation talk and memories of how things used to be. He told Nana, among other things, that he had been coming to this resort for many years. He paused a few minutes, looked up and down the crowded beach and then out at the swimmers diving into and hurdling against the white-foamed crests of the breaking waves, and said, "Things are changing now. I've noticed more of them in the last year or two."

Nana said nothing. She looked out at her grandchildren tugging and wrestling over the two rafts she had rented.

"They sure are closing in on us, aren't they?" he continued. "Look at those colored kids taking away that white boy's raft. The lifeguard ought to do something about that. Those people are just moving right in on us."

"Hmmm . . ." Nana murmured softly without making a comment. Just then, Malcolm—one of "those colored kids"—came hopping and bouncing over the knee-deep breakers toward his grandmother.

"Nana! Nana! They won't share! They won't give me a long turn on either one of the rafts," shouted Malcolm as he ran toward her. Very upset and about to cry, he stopped three or four feet short of Nana's blanket. The little guy, his well-built, dark-brown body wet and glistening, pointed toward his brother and sister, still in the water. He pleaded for adult intercession, in his favor, of course.

Nana stood up and prepared to take leave of the perplexed, gray-haired man, saying to him in a soft voice, "Excuse me, I think I can solve my grandson's problem." She took Malcolm by the hand and led him to the rental stand where she paid the deposit for a third raft. Malcolm dashed back to the water, smiling broadly, his raft—bigger than he—dragging behind him. Nana returned to her blanket. The chatty visitor was gone.

When Stanli and I joined Mother on the beach a short time thereafter, she laughingly told us about the man—her peer—who had met Malcolm's "white" grandmother.

We sensed that she was relieved to have us sitting with her. Now, all observers could readily tell that she had an affiliation with "those people" who some think "are moving right in." Stanli asked her how she really felt in situations like that. Mother was quick to reply.

"I'll tell you," she said. "I was rescued when Malcolm ran toward me yelling, 'Nana! Nana!' There were no nasty looks or bitter words as Malcolm and I, hand in hand, walked away from the stunned man. That walk told the story of how I fitted into the life on the beach—and a rapidly changing world—better than any words I could have mustered. No doubt, the man is hopping angry that I didn't tell him, when he first approached me, that I had so-called colored grandchildren."

Mother paused and looked at the children, now reconciled and floating happily on their rafts. "There is one thing that really bothers me," she continued. "It's something I feel strongly I don't have to do. I simply don't have to hang a sign from my neck stating that I'm a white grandmother in an interracial family or that one of my sons married a black woman."

In saying that, Mother recognized all too well that there were those who would like her to display such a sign. She recalled for us several occasions at conferences or luncheons where "rude, shameful remarks" were made by persons critical of interracial dating and marriages. The individuals making these attacks were at the time unaware of Mother's own interracial ties; a few of them were later apprised of "Mary Kae's black daughter-in-law." In one instance, a friend told Mother that someone else had thought it "totally unfair of Mary Kae not to inform the people sitting at the luncheon table of her interracial ties prior to the conversation," which had included racial slurs and indignities.

Imagine, for a moment, what this would sound like: "I'm pleased to meet you. I'm Mary Kae Becker. I'm a white grandmother. My older son married a black woman. They have five children of various colors. Please be guarded in your comments. I don't want you to think I'm unfair."

It is unlikely that Mother will ever hang a sign around her neck stating that she is a white grandmother with interracial ties. That is not her style. Being the patient woman that she is, her approach to the touchy situations she faces from time to time will undoubtedly remain low-keyed, characterized by calmness and control.

# 12

## *I Can't Wait*
### by Marquita

Almost always I have to go to the bathroom at different times than my brothers and sister. When Mom says, "Bathroom check!" before a trip, I can't go—not until we're in the car. I try to use the toilet before dinner, but I don't have to go until I start eating.

One hot evening after dinner, Mom took Martin, Malcolm, Meredith and me to the swimming pool. I was four years old. It was especially fun that night because we were the only big children at the whole pool. A baby was there, too, with his mother and father. Martin, Malcolm and Meredith used the bathroom at home, and I tried. I couldn't go. But as soon as my toes touched the cool water in the pool, I had to go.

"Mom, I have to go to the bathroom," I told her. She was just getting ready to sit in a lounge chair.

"Wouldn't you know," Mom said. "Come on. Let me get the lifeguard to keep an eye on the boys while we're gone. Meredith, you sit on the side until I get back, please!" Mom yelled to him.

I wasn't even wiggly as I followed Mom to the lifeguard's chair.

"Hi!" Mom said to the lifeguard. "I've got to take my little one to the bathroom." Mom pointed down at my head. "Would you be kind enough to watch my sons while we're gone? One is on the side over there." Mom pointed to Meredith, who was kicking his feet in the three-foot water. "The other two are in the twelve-foot section, jumping off the boards. It's okay. They're good swimmers."

Hurry up, Mommy, I was thinking. The lifeguard looked at the twelve-foot part, then at the three-foot part, and then at the twelve-foot part again. I didn't know what she was looking for. I could see Malcolm and Martin jumping off the two low diving boards at the same time, racing to different sides, running back to the boards and jumping in again. Nobody else was even in that deep part.

The lifeguard said to Mom, "Two? Where?"

I was ready to whine now. I was getting wiggly. How come that silly lifeguard couldn't see Malcolm's big, brown body and his big Afro and his light blue swimming trunks? Couldn't she see Martin on the other side? He had on his red trunks—the white string was hanging down his leg—and he kept rubbing his pink-tan chest and slinging the water out of his blond hair. Both of them were laughing, too. Mom always says not to call people "stupid"; but I thought the lifeguard was stupid, and I really wanted to go to the bathroom now!

Mom put her hands on her hips and gave the lifeguard her annoyed look.

"Well," said the lifeguard to Mom, "I see one . . ."

Which one couldn't she see, I wondered. I started wiggling badly. "Nooo," said Mom. "You see TWO!"

"Uuuuuh, yes, I guess I do," said the lifeguard softly.

"Maaammeeee! I gotta go! Maaa!" I shouted.

"Let's run, honey," Mom said and grabbed my hand.

"Whew!" I was glad Mommy remembered me. Next time I'll try harder at home, I thought as I barely made it.

# 13

## Pink-White Daddy and Brown-Black Son
### by Malcolm

One Saturday Dad took me to the shoe repair shop in the Shaker Square shopping area. He had to pick up some shoes for Mom. He also wanted to treat me to an ice cream cone for doing my work and staying out of trouble in school.

There are a lot of stores around Shaker Square. Dad says it's one of the oldest shopping centers in the country—maybe the oldest. It wasn't very busy. I usually see more people in the new shopping malls. I like the malls better. They have game rooms, ramps and twisting stairs to run up and down, and the malls aren't as old as the buildings at Shaker Square.

We walked by one man who kept staring at us. I was holding Dad's hand. I turned around and looked back at the man. He turned around, too, and looked at us again. I said to Dad, "That man is staring at us."

"What man, Malcolm?"

"That man back there." I pointed to the man.

"Put your hand down, Malcolm. You're asking for trouble when you point at people." Dad turned to look, but he didn't get very excited. He turned back, put his arm around me and hugged my shoulders. As we walked on to the shoe shop, I put my arm mostly around his waist—I was kind of tall even though I was six years old then. Before we went through the store doorway, I stopped and looked once more for that man. "He's still looking, Dad," I reported.

"Malcolm," said Dad, "I bet that man can't take his eyes off us because we're so good-looking, son." Then Dad laughed.

"Nope," I said. "I know why he's looking at us."

"Oh, you do, Malcolm? Why?"

"Because you're a pink-white daddy and I'm a brown-black son."

### THAT Black?

*"Black" is not THAT black.*
*Not carbon black. Inky-black?*
*Who is "as black as the ace of spades"?*
*"White" is not SO white.*
*Not chalk white. Not milky-white.*
*What "po' white cracker" is really white?*

                              Stanli and Tom Becker
                                  (May, 1981)

# 14

## *Blackness and Reality*
### by Stanli

Malcolm's brothers and sisters "crack up" when he says, "Don't worry about all that black and white stuff. That's stupid stuff! We're all human!" They love to hear Malcolm say this. Partly, it's because of the way he says it. Malcolm is dramatic and demonstrative. He is honest in his perceptions, and he says things in an open and sincere manner. For instance, when he told Tom that the man at Shaker Square was staring at them because Tom was a "pink-white daddy" and he was a "brown-black son," Malcolm brushed aside his dad's kidding remark that the man was staring at them because they were "so good-looking." We still laugh in amusement about the "pink-white daddy/brown-black son" comment, but we also recognize in Malcolm an intuitiveness and a maturity about humanness which seem lacking in many, many adults.

In a society where children are expected to conform their thinking to the notion of separate and distinct races, Tom and I are certain to be taken to task for encouraging our children to acknowledge the idea of "race" only for the myth that it is. We have obviously decided to accept that charge. More significant, though, is that Malcolm, at his young age, is determined to apply this belief.

At this point in his life, Malcolm is very aware of his

physical presence, and his self-identity includes acceptance of his mirror-image: flashing, big brown eyes (easily distorted into dramatically different expressions) set in a man-size face; dark brown, usually silky-smooth skin; thick, black, tightly curled hair, cut in a medium-size Afro-style; husky, slightly pot-bellied but muscular, strong, agile body. He knows he has a beautiful smile, an unpleasant whine, sometimes inappropriate tears and a good baseball arm. Himself he describes as "human," first, last and foremost. That he doesn't call himself "black" does not mean he lacks an understanding of what is meant by "black" or "white" in our society. He showed a keen awareness of these concepts when he referred to himself as a "brown-black son" and to Tom as a "pink-white daddy." Malcolm knows that most other people consider him "black" and his dad "white"; he is increasingly conscious of the stereotypes associated with both. Very carefully, he joined brown and pink with these concepts to indicate to Tom, and perhaps to himself, that his own beliefs and perception of people influence his observations and language. Thus, Malcolm, at age six, protected his developing values and self-concept from a staring man who, Malcolm thought, saw no more than a "black" boy and a "white" man walking together and holding hands. Malcolm does not allow "racial" divisiveness to come between himself and other members of his family, even through the eyes of observers. When he can share and extend this comprehension of humanness to his playmates and other adults, he does so with joy. Even in informal situations, Malcolm prefers that persons being discussed not be called "black" or "white"; he takes the time to describe individuals and encourages his friends to do the same. Yet, he is able to grasp the depth of feeling and meaning involved in the complex ways people deal with "race."

 I talk to my children about what it means to be called "black" and what is involved in calling one's self "black." I try to help them get the flavor of the range of games and pretenses complicating color coding among "blacks," "browns," and "whites." Difficult to explain is how people of various colors from other countries "fit" into American perceptions, both "black" and "white."

Further, and perhaps more essentially, I explore with the children the values and behaviors, positive and negative, which arise from the malady of "race-thinking." We discuss slavery, how it influenced people at different levels of society and in different geographical locations at that time, juxtaposing many of the results which still reverberate through today's America. They hear from me what growing up "black" in West Virginia meant in the 1940s and 1950s: attending segregated schools for most of my public schooling; not seeing Howdy Doody or Big John and Sparky "in person" at one of the local "white" theatres; not eating in restaurants until my late teen years; seeing the symphony orchestra from the balcony only, and more. I point out what it means for people to suffer—on various levels and to greater and lesser degrees—because their progress and opportunities are limited by being labeled "black" in the U.S.A.

I am careful, though, to contrast the spiritedness, the feelings, the fun, the normalcy of my early community life. I did experience the sense of being in the majority. Segregated schools, churches and organizations provided this awareness; there was freedom from the anxieties associated with constantly being a minority something-or-other. I began to realize how many, many people must be like myself, namely "colored," not "white." I started thinking about the numbers of "colored" peoples worldwide, surely constituting a majority. I was, in fact, a member of the world's nonwhite majority.

My young Beckers have learned from their Uncle Jan why he raised his clenched fist in the "Black Power" salute and why he has taught them the special hand greeting he uses instead of a simple handshake. They have discovered this as one way in which people who share like sentiments communicate with each other. This has led us to discussions about why people call themselves "black" and form organizations to deal with injustices and to promote equality as well as to support each other in the knowledge that all is not well and that changes must occur.

I elaborate on the obvious confusions and inconsistencies. How could I explain to the children that my mother (Gran, to them) and Aunt Belle called themselves "black" and yet had almost the same color complexion as Tom's parents? Why do people having the lightest of tan skins and those having the darkest of brown skins seem willing to call themselves "black"? I talk with the children about reality, leading to such considerations as "You're called black, Mom, right? But you're really brown."

"Right," I answer firmly, in this instance to Malcolm, glad to have proof of this depth of his thinking. A child like Malcolm would be so vulnerable—laughed at, ridiculed by his peers—if he didn't know and understand that he was viewed as "black" by most other people. So would his younger, dark, brown-skinned brother, Meredith. Malcolm's lighter, honey-brown and tan-skinned sisters, Monti and Marquita, and his majority-culture-skin-colored brother, Martin, would also be "up against it" day after day if they didn't understand how that "one black drop" rule plays the lead role in American racism.

The children also learn that there is far more to "blackness" than skin color. A primary focus for creating an appreciation of their rich heritage is an examination of black culture—its genesis, history, beauty, durability and its great strength. Many of the notable ideals and goals of the black culture are stated in the documents that frame the U.S. ideology but seem more magnified through the compassionate consciousness of "actions speaking louder than words" in the subcultures of sufferers. The traditional association of "blacks" and "Jews" exemplifies this reality; a look at the subcultures of the Irish, Italians and other immigrant groups in this country shows this at a different level.

Prominently displayed on a shelf of our living room library stands W. E. B. DuBois' *Black Reconstruction in America*, a book given to my grandmother as a gift, then passed on to me. My grandmother Emma Wade Hamler was a librarian and a graduate of the first four-year class from West Virginia State College. She had to work as a domestic to earn the money to put her two daughters through college. Not bitter, she resumed her professional career when librarian positions became available again in the late thirties. She was a librarian at Garnet Branch Library, located in Charleston's Negro high school. I can remember sitting at the low, round tables with little chairs circling them. I was proud to have read or been read all the books for little children. I have fond memories of lunches with Mrs. Spurlock and Granny in their back room office. I didn't know then that my grandmother was working behind the scenes to integrate the so-called public library—the ivy-covered building we stood in front of to catch the bus to go home from shopping.

One day, Granny took me to the top of the winding stone steps leading to the doors of that library. For Granny, physically climbing those steps was an undertaking in itself; she had become increasingly crippled by multiple sclerosis. I didn't know, when she checked out a book for me that day, that I could not yet go in and sit at a table and read as I did at Garnet Branch. That we could then even enter the door of the main *public* library and request a book to take out was due in great part to Granny's own labors. I've been told that taking me on that trip up those winding stone steps was one of the highpoints of her life. Maybe that's why DuBois' *Black Reconstruction in America* and a few others of Granny's prized books were passed on to me. That symbolic book, with its worn and faded brown cover, for me, tells a story of "black" heritage. One thing is for certain: this story has been passed on to my children.

In these bookcases, the children can also reach for Alex Haley's *Roots*, the *Autobiography of Malcolm X*, a collection of essays called *The Black Power Revolt*, or various works by James Baldwin, Nikki Giovanni, J. A. Rogers and others. On a low shelf within easy reach of the little ones is *Little Brown Baby: Paul Laurence Dunbar, Poems for Young People* by Bertha Rodgers.[25] Each of my children has taken his or her turn on my lap with big smiles and giggles as I've recited "Little Brown Baby," or read "When a Feller's Itchin' to be Spanked," "The Boogah Man" and others. Next to this favorite book, the older children can finger the poems of Langston Hughes and thereby reach back into history to taste of the Harlem Renaissance. They can also learn about the ways of South Side Chicago from that famous black poet Gwendolyn Brooks. They have met her, this Pulitzer Prize winner. They proudly take their relatives and friends to a photo collage hanging in our front hall to view the snapshot of them sitting with Miss Brooks.

The works of Gwendolyn Brooks occupy a special place in one bookcase. She has autographed them and even made marginal notes in some. Placed with this outstanding poet's works is my own master's thesis in which I humbly attempted to capture the early development of Miss Brooks and her initial works.

I believe that my children understand why I feel strongly about, feel proud of my black culture. They know also how vehemently I feel about the urgent need to reject the mythology of "race" and to fight against the ills it casts upon society. Tom joins me in refuting the concept of separate and distinct "races," but, to do so, he does not find it necessary to deny his "Irish-German-American" heritage.

When I reflect upon my Afro-American heritage, the roots of my "black experience," I see my crippled grandmother as she slowly accompanied me up those winding stone steps to the *public* library in Charleston, West Virginia. I can sit in my living room and look at Granny's old books with frayed edges and faded colors. I still see the younger of my two brothers, George, portraying black Revolutionary War hero Crispus Attucks, fall "dead" on the steps of the First Baptist Church; I recall my third grade class dressed as slaves to celebrate the black spirituals during one Negro history week. I hear echoes of Mama playing the piano and singing, as she taught us children the words to "Lift Every Voice and Sing." I can read about the Harlem Renaissance and still hear the verses I joined others in reciting, sitting in the front row of the dilapidated auditorium of my segregated school—front row, only because that row was reserved for first graders. The pulsations of fury still pound through my blood when I think back to the six-foot chain link fence topped with barbed wire, which was implanted around the lunch counter *inside* a downtown department store during the early sit-ins of the 1960s in Charleston.

There have been, however, some significant adjustments in my thinking and behavior regarding my "black" identity precisely because of my "interracial" family and our experiences. I don't remember the exact day, or the time of day, when I stopped thinking of Tom as "white," when I thought of classifications. That's not the way the mind works, anyhow. That processing followed, in the passage of time, after those heated words between Tom and me at that late night dinner in 1971, about four years after we had been married; Tom had vehemently challenged my long-held assumption that our daughter was to be called "black."

Neither does Tom remember when he stopped regarding me as a member of the "black race." But each of us did change our thinking. The entire idea of separate and distinct "races" became an absurdity which could no longer be a part of our lives. We spoke to our children of humanness, of the one human family to which all people belong. This became the foundation upon which our values, attitudes, and beliefs—our family philosophy—has been built and nurtured.

I began to take more notice of the kinds of forms I was requested to fill in, first as part of my graduate studies, then for employment, and so on. Soon, I found myself refusing to indicate my "race" on forms which had no appropriate line, box or circle whereby my children could declare their "interracialness," were they old enough and inclined to do so. I once said something about this issue to a top administrator of a university where I did graduate work. He gave me "a song and dance" about federal forms and their requirements. Precisely this kind of malarky nourishes the myth of separate and distinct races in our society. The teachers, school administrators, census takers and others who explain "race" through this "mumbo-jumbo" become, in effect, the perpetuators and protectors of the myth. The harm which results from lumping people into "races," for whatever reasons, has long been recognized. Yet, the practice continues, and the dangers mount. Paul R. Ehrlich and S. Shirley Feldman appeal to Americans to recognize the perils of "race-thinking" and to defuse the "race bomb" in their book *The Race Bomb: Skin Color, Prejudice, and Intelligence.* Not to do so soon, they predict, is to "help push civilization toward the brink of catastrophe."[26]

As the 1980 census neared, Tom and I knew that we would not darken the circles next to "White" and "Black or Negro," as they were to be worded. At about that time, I received from Gwendolyn Brooks her 1980 pamphlet *Primer for Blacks,* published by the Black Position Press.[27] She is one of the articulators of "blackness" whom I greatly respect. I love her; for me, she represents much of what black culture is about as she writes of the sights, sounds and odors, the thoughts, frustrations and contemplations, and the universals from her perspective. I read, then shared with Tom, her writing about "Blackness"—its defense, its definition, its clarification. We discussed Miss Brooks' views on "Black Validation" and the need for an "essential Black statement . . . not dulled by assimilationist urges, secret or overt."[28] We talked about and deliberated upon these ideas late into the night; yet, I knew what I had to do; we knew what we had to do.

For Tom not to fill in the circle next to "white" was quite a different matter than for me to choose not to fill in the circle next to "black." Tom readily admits to have given almost no thought to the category "white" as he marked the circle or checked the box next to it on form after form throughout the greater part of his life. He grew up in America's "white world"; for Tom, checking or circling "white" just seemed to be an expected response in the officialese of the many forms, surveys and applications which had become a routine of life. Completing the "race" item meant no more to him than providing information about sex, weight, hair and eyes on his driver's license application.

If Tom had lingered over any item, it was color of eyes. At present, the description on his driver's license reads "blue." Over the years, however, on the eleven or twelve operator's licenses issued to him, he has described his eyes also as green, blue-green, blue-gray, and even green-gray. As a new driver in 1949, he left this item blank and asked the lady at the application counter to assist him in this decision, as he smiled and pointed to the sign on the wall behind her, ASK FOR ASSISTANCE HERE. She did. Tom doesn't remember which of the above colors she chose, but both he and the lady laughed about the otherwise dull procedure.

Not all Americans routinely darkened those circles or marked those boxes next to "racial" categories as did

Tom for so many years, without giving thought to the matter. A friend dining at our home once shared with us how she entered a prestigious midwestern university as "black" and graduated two years later as "Hispanic." When Selina entered the university, "Hispanic" was not one of the choices on the form provided her. "I chose black at that time," said Selina, "because I considered myself as a Puerto Rican of color. After all, my skin is similar in color to many people in America who identify as black." Physical coloring was the basis for her decision.

Because of increasing government and foundation interest in minority enrollment—and because money became available for special categories of students—this university joined hundreds of other educational institutions in revising their application and financial aid forms. The category "Hispanic" was added to the form provided by Selina's university as she prepared to graduate. Suddenly, she was faced with a choice between "black" and "Hispanic" since it was clearly stated to check only one item. "What really frustrated me," recounted Selina, "is that I was told I would have to choose between black and Hispanic. I tried to point out the fallacy of a policy that holds that one can claim only a part of one's identity on these forms, but I did so to no avail."

"Hispanic" was more descriptive of the culture with which Selina identified; her parents were from Puerto Rico. Her selection at graduation on the revised form was, therefore, "Hispanic."

"Well, let me tell you what happened to me," said her husband, Joe, "when I was being processed for admission to Aviation Cadet School in the Air Force back in the 1940s." He paused for a moment . . ."I was among the first minority cadets to be accepted into this kind of training." Joe looked at Tom, then at me, and said, "I don't know if you are aware that my father was black and my mother was white."

Tom and I had known Joe and Selina for eight years, but, shaking our heads, we indicated to Joe that he had just revealed something new to us.

"You know the many forms you have to plow through in the service . . . that's what I was doing," Joe went on.

"How well I remember," Tom added.

Joe smiled, looked to Tom, and said, "I bet this didn't happen to you." Joe chuckled before continuing. "There was this white sergeant. His job was to go over those forms to make sure they were filled in correctly. He gave my forms the same attention as the others . . . that is, until he came upon the box entitled 'Race,' in which I had written Mulatto. I had already given a lot of thought to this, and I had decided that, for me, it was quite accurate. Mulatto was a designation which, to me, recognized the significant role my white mother played in my life. She was the one who reared me in the absence of my father. The sergeant looked up at me; then, as quickly as he could look down and find the right box again, he boldly struck out Mulatto and wrote in Negro."

Joe was right; not this, nor anything approaching it, had happened to Tom during his Army days. That the color of his eyes was the only physical feature he ever paused to think about in completing all those forms throughout his lifetime is testimony to the psychological security afforded to "whites" as they grow up to fit into "white" America as members of the majority-skin-color culture.

The 1980 census would mark for Tom the beginning of his fiftieth year. For the very first time in his life, the "race" item posed a problem for him. Tom had already told me that "it just wouldn't be right for me [Tom] to continue marking white." The children, for some years now, had called him a "human being" of the colors pink, tan, and yellow . . . "kind of red" at times. They called him red, sometimes rosy, because of his dermatographia—a condition of the skin whereby rubbing the skin produces a redness which will last for some time. Inasmuch as this is not a serious medical disorder, and since it caused no pain to Tom, he sometimes allowed the children to write and draw on his arms, neck and back with their fingers or pencil erasers. They found great delight in watching the letters and designs they made gradually become red and remain visible for several minutes or more.

Tom knew that he could no longer check the box next to "White" in question four on the census questionnaire. The 1980 census, for Tom, would not be the conventional form-filling exercise of the past.

I knew, as did Tom, that I would choose not to check the circle beside "Black or Negro," even though "black" is descriptive of a basic and unchanged part of my identity. Always and forever will my Afro-American heritage—the experience of "Blackness"—be a part of me and whatever else I am or become. It is only by accepting it—loving it—that I am enabled to grow, to broaden the context of my life.

# 15

## *Call Me Human*
**by Tom**

An afternoon chat with Edward and Louise Hope over tea or coffee had become a seize-the-present-hour pleasure for Stanli and me. On one of these occasions several years ago, Ed handed us a single sheet of paper with a poem on it.

"This is one of many poems written by my late wife," he said. "It is unpublished. One of my present goals is to assemble this one and some others and have them printed so that I can donate them to a college, where they might be used in some way to generate a scholarship fund in her name. But I want to share this particular one with you and Stanli. You may be able to use it. I hope so."

**Call Me Human
Why Label Me?**

*If you want to call me African, European, Indian-
   American
Since my roots too are all three,
Save your breath.*

*Use your knowledge and your strength*
*To break down barriers that you have made*
*To keep men apart.*

*Jensen and Shockley, stop saying*
*I can't learn, think and grow.*
*Instead let it be known that all people*
*Have common needs and are different branches of*
*One Family.*

*Religion, Education, and Politics, you have used*
*To condition my mind.*
*In the library I learned other facts*
*About the strengths and frailties of all*
*All mankind.*

*Rewrite your biased history books and include*
*What all men (black, red, brown, white and yellow)*
*Have added to the world's storehouse of knowl-*
*edge*
*And show how that knowledge can better serve*
*People everywhere.*

*Remove your prejudiced blinders and you can't*
*help but see*
*That we are true members of*
*The Human Family.*

*Why waste time trying to find a label*
*To pin on me*
*Since all I need is*
*Opportunity.*

Marion Conover Hope
(January, 1974)

Stanli and I agreed that we would have to make a statement to this effect in the approaching 1980 census. We were to be "write-ins"!

Call us human! Marion Conover Hope spoke for us Beckers each when she wrote, "Why label me?"

# 16

## Computers Don't Take Human
by Tom

"Marquita, will you count the people in our family?" I asked, knowing that on good days she could count all the way to 20.

"One . . ." she said, pausing and pointing to Malcolm sitting across from her in the circle. "Two . . ." she continued, smiling, her finger jumping back to Meredith on her side of the circle. The children giggled, knowing that Marquita's style was not to proceed around the circle in orderly fashion as adults are wont to do. Four-year-old Marquita finally reached "seven," pointing to herself and adding, "There!" Her counting recitals always won over our young audience and put them in good humor. We had a positive beginning.

Monti had asked if she could fill in the sample census questionnaire worksheet which her mother had brought home. Stanli had been appointed to the Mayor of Cleveland's 1980 (Census) Complete Count Executive Committee. As a result, she brought home many useful blurbs and fliers from the U.S. Department of Commerce.

"Where do I write the '7,' Mom?" asked our eager, young recorder.

"We don't actually write the '7,'" answered Stanli. "We asked Marquita to count us so we would know how many of these boxes our family needs to fill in." In truth, Marquita had been asked to count because of the parents' desire for a good start to this family conference. Stanli moved her finger across the column of boxes on the census questionnaire, showing them to the children. "We need seven."

Marquita smiled. "Seven" had been her contribution.

"Here's the place for our names," said Stanli. "Let's begin with Dad. What is your last name?"

"Becker."

"Your first name?"

"John."

"Your middle initial?"

"T."

" 'T' is for Tom," added Malcolm.

"Thomas," Martin corrected.

The children provided information about their names, each adding some tidbits of interest about her or his name. Stanli and I had conspired carefully for our "Census '80 family circle." Through past experience we knew that our children would pay attention to discussions about their own names.

"Why did I get this name?"

"I want a different name, like 'Michelle'!"

"I'm going to change my name when I get older."

"Who am I named after?"

"My name stinks!"

"Am I named for anybody?"

Question 1 proved to be a good point of departure. To keep things moving, our scheme called for discussion of Question 3—Sex and Question 6—Marital Status.

"Sex is the next item," said Stanli. "We are asked to fill in either male or female."

Marquita and Meredith, who still did not discriminate much between boy-type playthings and girl-type playthings, looked on as the older ones went into the giggling and wiggling acts so well-known to parents and teachers. The mere mention of the word "sex" turns elementary school kids into squirmy, giddy little monkeys. But the subject does capture their attention, and that's precisely what my wife and I wanted.

I looked at the older ones. "We're not going into all the questions about sex today." They knew that Stanli and I were very open and frank about sex questions; that aspect of their education was still primarily a family affair. Our schools initiated "sex education" in the fifth grade. However, discussions about sex began long before the fifth grade—on the sidewalks and street corners between school and home. That's why we made it a family affair from their earliest years.

"We just need to say whether each of us is male or female," said Stanli. "Are you a boy or girl, Marquita?"

"I'm a girl!" shrieked Marquita, now caught up in the giggling and wriggling.

Monti, the last to answer, uttered a sophisticated "Female" as she filled in the circle in her box.

"Now . . . marital status . . . how many of you are married?" Stanli asked with the straight face of a poker player.

"Married, ugh!"

"Not me . . . no way!"

"I hate girls!"

"Nope!" said another.

"Oh, c'mon Mom, just you and Dad are married," said Monti, smiling broadly, eager to resume her recording.

All of us burst into laughter. At least the children were having some fun in this family discussion. For some time now our older ones had not huddled around our circles with the same enthusiasm shown in their younger years. Then, discussions had often centered upon organizing picnics, planning trips, telling and reading stories and those sorts of things. Meredith and Marquita still showed interest in these topics, but the older ones had become frequently present in body but not mind. They had many other preferred activities: roller-skating, ice-skating, go-cart construction, bike-riding, fishing, soccer, hockey, baseball and more. In contrast, family circles which focused on "home duties," "keeping rooms clean," or "too much fighting and arguing" became harsh examples of children held in captivity—even if only for fifteen to twenty minutes. My wife and I had undertaken to set firm ground rules to insure cooperation during these group conferences, such as "No one goes out to play until the discussion is completed . . . and completed to everyone's satisfaction." ("Everyone" meant Mom and Dad, and all the children knew it.) Our discussion about the U.S. census was blossoming into one of our bigger, recent successes. Not once did we say, "No one goes out to play until. . . ."

The children's facts-of-life demonstration had eased into the whispering stage, when they edged up to each other with cupped hands covering lips and ears as they traded off the "facts." Stanli took advantage of this situation to introduce the fourth item on the census questionnaire. "In this box we are asked to indicate what we are," she said, pointing to all the choices. "Listed are White, Black or Negro, Japanese, Chinese, Indian and some others."

"Hmmm . . ." I murmured, looking at Stanli, then at the children. "I might have a problem with this box."

"I know," said Malcolm, giggling again, "because I bet they don't have a pink daddy in that box."

"Ha . . . ha . . . ha," I said pokily, "and I bet, Malcolm, that they don't have a brown son in that box either."

Monti, in possession of the questionnaire worksheet once again, studied all fifteen categories and observed, "It doesn't say 'biracial' or 'mixed' anywhere here."

"That's dumb," added Martin.

"Monti, what is the last category in the box?" I asked.

"'Other,'" she replied. "It has the word 'Specify' next to it with an arrow pointing down."

"If you choose, honey, you may fill in the circle next to 'Other' and write 'biracial' or 'mixed' where the arrow is pointing," I said.

"Well, that's what I'm going to do," said Monti in a decisive tone. "I am, too," followed Martin.

"That makes three of us then," I added. "But I'm not going to write in pink, rosy or tan!"

"I'm black," interjected Meredith.

"Be quiet, Meredith, you don't know anything!" retorted Malcolm.

"Yes, I am black," said Meredith. "Henry said so!"

"Henry!" exclaimed Martin. "He's not even five years old. What does he know about anything? Do you remember all our family talks?"

"Family," said Stanli, "why don't we fill in the circle next to 'Other' for each of us? That appears to be the most honest choice we can make. We can write that we are a 'biracial' or 'interracial' family, and that we are, above all, of the human 'race'." Mom, who had just been appointed to the Mayor's Committee, seemed to have the answer.

"Yeah!" "That's what I want." "Me, too!" came the unanimous assent. Marquita and Meredith were caught in this contagion of responses.

With that acclamation, the "Census '80 family circle" adjourned. Off went the children to play. Monti remained behind to fill in the circles next to "Other"; under the arrow by "Specify" she wrote, "We are a biracial/multiracial family and identify as human." It was done! The census form was mailed on the following day.

Comments had already refocused on fun. "Dad, will you get our bikes out?" With this perennial query, I knew it was time to poke through the leaves in the yard for signs of tulip shoots. Gardening is one of the pleasanter adult activities in this family, especially when the children are on their bikes and out of shouting range. One of the first rites of spring for me is to climb to the storage floor atop the garage and bring down the bikes and trikes.

Shortly thereafter, Grandmother "Nana" Becker arrived to visit for two weeks. The solid, milk-chocolate rabbits she handed to her grandchildren launched the Easter celebrations earlier than Stanli and I had planned.

"That's what grandmothers are for," Nana said. "We do things for the children which parents won't or can't do." Of course, the children agreed, and the battle of how to eat and where to keep the large, messy, chocolate, candy rabbits began!

Several weeks had passed since our family conference on the Census '80 questionnaire. There had been very little talk about the census around home during these weeks. Stanli and I had commented to each other about the extensive news coverage being given to suspected undercounts in large metropolitan areas. This was one of Stanli's major concerns as a member of the Mayor's Committee. Little did we realize that our family was a part of that undercount.

This news first came to us through my mother who had taken a telephone call from a census worker. Neither Stanli nor I was home at the time. "There seems to be a problem," said Nana, "something about not having received your census form. The woman left a number to call."

I returned the call. The lady was a temporary, part-time worker for the 1980 census. Her job was to collect information about people in designated areas. Our name had been given to her, she believed, because our census questionnaire had not been received. I assured her that our form had been completed and mailed and that perhaps she ought to check again with her district office. She insisted that she needed the information immediately to meet her time deadlines. I could appreciate the lady's position; she was only doing her job. She offered to come to our home and assist us in filling out the form.

"No," I replied. "That is a family matter with us. You may drop the form off at our house today, if you wish, and we will complete it tonight. It will be mailed first thing in the morning."

She told me that she had to collect these forms herself. "Fine," I replied. "You may pick up the form yourself anytime tomorrow."

Our telephone conversation ended on a very polite note. This woman sounded like a person eager to carry out her responsibilities. Quite possibly our census return had been lost in the mail or misplaced among the hundreds of thousands of others being sorted. In good humor, I had mentioned to the lady that my wife was a member of the Mayor's Complete Count Executive Committee, and that we, especially, didn't want to be part of the undercount. Anyhow, this was only a once-every-ten-years inconvenience.

The woman picked up the completed census form the next day. She didn't even enter the house. This transaction took less time than it takes to pay the newspaper girl. I gave no further thought to the matter until dinner that evening when my mother cast a few clouds of suspicion upon the census takers. "Do you really think your first census form was lost? Or misplaced?" she asked. "Maybe they didn't believe what they saw on the first one." The amused look on Mother's face told me also that the children had shared their Census '80 decision-making with her. I knew what Mother was implying. Neither could she believe all that she saw and heard on her visits with us: the brown-black mother, the pink-white daddy, kids of deep brown and ebony, honey-brown, creamy-white and yellow-tan skins. More than once, Nana had to defend her own chosen identity: "Yes, I am white. I am proud to be white! I am a white grandmother!"

Had Nana extended her visit a few more weeks, she could have said, "I told you so." For we did receive another call from the census takers. The conversation went something like this:

| | |
|---|---|
| Census Taker: | Hello, I'm _____ . I'm calling for the census. We have received your form. Thank you. But there is still some information we need, and perhaps I can help you with it. |
| Tom: | Certainly. |
| Census Taker: | On item four, the whole family filled in the circles next to 'Other.' Can you be more specific . . . like black or white or another if appropriate? |
| Tom: | No, what we've written is as specific as we can be . . . and still be honest about it. We did add that we are a 'multiracial' family and that each of us identifies as 'human.' |
| Census Taker: | I understand. I'm familiar with mixed racial families, and I think I know how you feel about it. The difficulty is that our computers don't take 'human.' |
| Tom: | Your computers will do what humans tell them to do, madam. You need to reprogram your computers so that they can accept humans of mixed origins. |
| Census Taker: | I can't do that, sir. I'm not trying to offend you. I'm just trying to do my job as I've been asked to do it. Don't you lean a little one way or the other . . . like black or white or one of the other choices? |
| Tom: | No. We don't 'lean.' What we've written is quite accurate for our family. We gave considerable thought to our answers. As far as I'm concerned, any changes made will be of your doing. Or, if I have any further involvement, they will be made in a court of law. I think we've talked enough now. |
| Census Taker: | Thank you, sir. |

I hung up the phone. "Isn't that something," I said to myself. "Don't I 'lean' a little one way or the other?" Indeed, the 1980 census had not been the usual form-filling routine for me.

# 17

## *The Marshal Never Came*
by Monti

I was nine years old and in the fourth grade at the time of the 1980 census. I remember how Dad grumbled when he had to complete the second census form. He let me help him. I guess that's why Dad told me about the phone call he had received from the census office. I was a little frightened. "Do you think they might make us do it a third time, Dad? . . . their way?"

"No . . . no, we won't hear from them, again."

"But what if they send the police or sheriff or somebody and make us answer black or white? Could they put us in jail or something like that?"

Dad laughed. "Honey, the last thing the law wants to do is to put a nine-year-old girl in jail. As for me . . . well, they have a lot of things on their minds other than chasing me to find out which way I 'lean.'"

"What do you mean by 'lean,' Dad?"

"Well, the census worker asked me on the phone yesterday," he answered, "don't I 'lean' toward black or white?"

"Oh," I mumbled. Dad was getting ready to trim his beard and to shower. He kept talking. He talks to himself a lot when he's in the bathroom. The whole family knows that he talks to himself, too. Sometimes Mom will ask, "Tom, are you talking to me?" "No," he answers, "but you're welcome to listen if you want to." Dad was a college professor for years, and I think he liked to practice his lectures in the shower or bathtub. I followed him to the bathroom. There was something on my mind I wanted to ask him.

"Don't worry about the census form, the police, or the sheriff, Monti," he said, before I could ask my question. "That's not how the law works. There's still something called free speech in this country." Dad went on to tell me how federal marshals were used in the earliest censuses. They were called enumerators, and they decided what "race" a person belonged to—not the person, herself, as it is today. He said that there was even a category for slaves in the 1790 census. Dad and Mom had read a lot about the census. I guess that's because Mom was on the Mayor's census committee. Dad also told me that there was no record of anyone having been put in jail for not answering census questions or not answering them in a certain way. I felt better, but I still hoped Dad was right about a marshal or somebody else not coming to our home.

"Dad, what do you think I should tell other kids when they ask me what I am?" I finally asked my question.

"Honey, that's a decision you have to make."

I wasn't really surprised at Dad's answer, but I coaxed him further. "C'mon Dad, tell me what you would say. Sometimes I'm really not sure."

"Whew . . ." Dad took a deep breath. He set his shaving stuff on the sink and sat down on the bathroom stool. "Monti, many people will look upon you as 'black,' especially if they know Mom and me. That's the way it's been since the 1920 census. Before that time, children born of 'black' and 'white' parents were often referred to as 'mulattoes' and counted as such in the censuses."

"Is 'mulatto' like 'biracial,' Dad?"

"Yes."

"Well, why did they stop doing it like that, Dad?"

"Who really knows? Some said it became too difficult

to tell the difference between 'mulattoes' and some 'blacks' and 'whites.' That must have bothered quite a number of people—especially those 'whites' who wanted solely to believe in and see 'pure white' people. After the 1920 census, the category 'Mulatto' was dropped. Thereafter, there were to be 'black' people and 'white' people only."

"But Dad, that's stupid. Anyone can walk down the street and point out people who are biracial."

"No, honey . . . not anyone. Some people see just what they want to see, regardless of the facts before them. There are 'white' people who can look directly at a 'biracial' or 'multiracial' person and see only 'black.' They don't want to see any 'white' in the person, even though it's there. A large number of 'black' people think the same way."

"Sometimes I don't understand how adults think. They tell kids to be honest, and then they aren't honest! They tell kids to be fair, and then they aren't fair!"

Dad laughed. "Whoa, Monti. I'm an adult. Your mom is an adult. We're trying to be fair. You can't say that about ALL adults any more than I can say that ALL 'white' people look at a biracial child and see only 'black.' Get my point?"

I nodded and giggled along with Dad, but I still thought that adults do some pretty dumb things. "But Dad, you haven't answered my question. What do you think I should call myself?"

"If I don't answer that one, honey, you're going to accuse me of being unfair, right?"

"Yep, I sure will!"

"Okay, I already said that some people are going to call you 'black,' right?"

"Yep," I said again, trying to find Dad's answer.

"But," he continued, "you've got a solid claim to being 'white,' too. You know that I, of all people, believe that!" Dad smiled and winked at me. "After all, you are the child of a so-called black person and a so-called white person. And the way I see it, one half is as good as the other half. You can call yourself biracial, but a lot of children won't know what that means. You would have some explaining to do. At least, I think so. I don't know for sure. You fourth graders are more sophisticated than I was at your age."

"C'mon, Dad. Don't be ol' fashioned." We both laughed. Dad hadn't really helped that much, but I think we both shared the same feelings about what "biracial" meant to us. That's what we had written on our census questionnaire. "Biracial," or even "mixed," does let me be part of both my mom and dad; after all, that's just telling it like it is.

Dad was right; no federal marshal ever showed up to put us in jail. If one had come, though, I was ready. I would have shown him or her the two certificates of appreciation that Mom received. One was from the Mayor of Cleveland for her work on the Complete Count Committee, and the other was from the Secretary of the U. S. Department of Commerce for "outstanding cooperation in advancing public understanding of the 1980 Census of Population and Housing." After all, we just needed a little understanding ourselves.

# 18

## *They Don't Count Me*
### by Martin

My sister Monti was in a play at school. She was ten when she was in the fifth grade play *The Wizard of Oz*. Our whole family went to see it. Cousin Tia, Aunt Marci, Aunt Henrietta and Uncle Roscoe came to see her. We were excited. The children changed some of the play and sang a few songs from *The Wiz*.

The costumes were really neat. Monti was the Lion, and she was good, too! Mom made a long fur mane that covered Monti's hair and a furry tail that almost touched her ankles. Then Mom sewed fur mittens and fur foot covers. Monti got to wear a tan body suit and Mom's pantyhose. The best costume of all was the Tin Woodwoman's. I think her father worked for an air conditioning company, and hers was real metal! I felt it after the play.

About two months after the play, Monti brought home a school magazine. Her picture was in it. She was in her Lion costume. Dorothy, the Scarecrow and the Tin Woodwoman were in the same picture. It was in color, too. The name of the school magazine was *The Schools of Shaker Heights: everyone a winner!*[29] Mom and Dad told me that it was the 1980-81 annual report of our school system. I already knew that because I could read almost every word of it. I took it to bed with me. That's where I do most of my reading at home. I learned to read before I started school. I taught myself to read by taking easy books to bed at night. It was fun then. I still take good books and magazines to bed with me, especially if they are about fishing or hockey.

The morning after I read the report, I told Mom and Dad that there was something wrong in it. They looked at each other before they asked me what it was. "Monti and I are not in there," I told them.

"What do you mean, Marty?" Mom asked.

"Here it is! Look at this . . . on page 18. Here are the names of all the schools in Shaker Heights down the side. Then, look at these: Black, White, Hispanic, American Indian, Asian. They divide kids into races. Where am I? Where's Monti? They don't even have a place for kids who don't fit into just one race. Biracial kids aren't in here! It's not like the census. There was a place for me in the census." I was sure I was right.

"Well, Marty, they probably counted you by their system. Someone put each of you into one of these categories, 'Black' or 'White,' and, in your case, we don't know which one." Mom looked thoughtful.

"But nobody asked me how I wanted to be counted," I said. "That's not right."

"You know what, Marty?" said Dad. "I think there are some errors in that report." Mom nodded her head, agreeing with Dad.

"Marty, hand me the calculator, please?" Mom asked. "Let's do some math with this report." She ran her finger across some numbers on the page and punched them on the calculator. "The total for male and female is the same as the total for those five categories. That means that each child who goes to school has been made to fit into one of those groups, whether it's right or not." Mom was talking seriously.

"If they put Monti's picture in there, and almost everybody at school knows you and Dad from PTA and stuff, how did they count her?" I really didn't understand this. Monti must be counted a little bit differently. But there weren't any one-halves in those numbers on page 18.

"Remember how we've had plenty of discussions about the way most people think and about how they classify others by skin color?" Yes, I nodded my head. Dad went on, "Well, Monti's skin is light brown and tan, almost cinnamon-like in the summer. Most people in this country would call her black on that basis alone."

"You understand how silly that is," said Mom softly, "but for sure she's counted under that 'black' heading in the report." I moved to sit on her lap.

"What about me?" I asked. "If Monti and I are both biracial, am I in the black total, too? I know people at school who think I'm white." Mom and Dad had explained to me long ago about my mirror image being what most people call white. But I knew that people who looked like Mom and Dad were responsible for my birth. "I'm not one or the other. I'm both, and I don't want to be called black or white." I really felt sad. "It's not fair. I'm both!"

"We know you are, Marty," said Dad. "Think back to the census last year when everybody in the family agreed that no one is black or white, but that all of us are human. Our skins are different colors, and we probably have lots of different mixtures in our backgrounds. That's why we decided to fill in the circle next to 'Other.' Then we wrote biracial or multiracial. We knew it was the right thing for us to do. We know from our own family how people are many different mixes and how that doesn't matter with us."

"I wish school was like our home, but it isn't." I put my arm around Mom's neck when I said this. "Maybe I should go to a private school where things are fair, and you can be what you want to be."

"Nope! You would probably find the same thing there," said Mom. "But you know we love you and that you can make your own decision about what you call yourself and stand by it. Dad and I will support you."

"Then I guess I better tell the school that everyone is not a winner, no matter what the annual report says." I hopped up, hugged Mom, then Dad, and went to get dressed. "Could I have my breakfast in a minute?" I headed up the stairs to my room. I knew Mom and Dad would know what to do.

# 19

## *Mixed Origins*
### by Stanli

During the 1950s, 1960s and 1970s, scientific racism encountered rough waters. Efforts to divide people into separate biological groupings called "races" ran aground and now apparently lay stranded. In 1980, even the U. S. Census Bureau dropped the term "race" from the census questionnaire. Respondents that year were asked to identify themselves by choosing among fourteen listed "racial/ethnic" categories. A fifteenth category, designated "Other—Specify," provided one more option to the already listed choices.

In spite of what might be called "relaxed" criteria for the country as a whole, it seems ironic that the nation's agency for education, the U. S. Department of Education, through its *School System Summary Report*, collects what it calls "racial/ethnic" data on school children in a rigid, five category system: (1) Black, (2) White, (3) American Indian or Alaskan, (4) Asian or Pacific Islander and (5) Hispanic.[30] The system is inflexible; there is no other choice, no category labelled "Other," no "Mixed," no "Exceptions," no "Combinations." School districts have no way to report children with "mixed" origins to the Department of Education.

This bureaucracy for education is quick to acknowledge on this unbending, five-category instrument that its "racial/ethnic designations . . . do NOT denote scientific definitions of anthropological origins."[31] Scientific or not, the given definitions of "Black" and "White" do indeed refer to origins.

> Black, Not of Hispanic Origin: A person having <u>origins</u> in any of the Black racial groups of Africa. (Underlining mine.)

> White, Not of Hispanic Origin: A person having <u>origins</u> in any of the original peoples of Europe, North Africa, or the Middle East. (Underlining mine.)[32]

How school personnel are to use these definitions in a nonscientific manner to determine "racial/ethnic" origins is not clarified in the instructions, unless teachers and principals resort to the following: "for the purposes of this report, a pupil may be included in the group to which he or she appears to belong, identifies with, or is regarded in the community as belonging to. However, no person should be counted in more than one racial/ethnic category."[33] The latter statement flies in the face of those many anthropologists who point out that most persons are of mixed racial/ethnic origins.

In the case of a child born of one "black" parent and one "white" parent, the U. S. Department of Education provides no other directions for teachers and school administrators on how to choose between the "black" origins and the "white" origins for reporting purposes. One additional recourse would be to refer to 1978 Federal Register Directive 15 which states that "the category which most clearly reflects the individual's recognition in his community should be used for purposes of reporting on persons who are of mixed racial and/or ethnic origins."[34] Again, as in the *School System Summary Report*, this Directive continues to muddle matters by "passing the buck" to the community. One might wonder why the 1978 Federal Directive and the Department of Education's *Report* refer to a child's "origins" at all in defining "black" or "white" or any other category; for, how a person is perceived in his or her community obviously takes precedence. It is unlikely that people in communities throughout the nation are aware that they have this responsibility. I believe that there are some communities in this country which would recognize the right of children to claim all of their origins.

In many more U. S. communities, certainly, the thinking of the citizenry is not yet far removed from that of the early colonial plantation owners. In the 1660s, Maryland and Virginia enacted state laws placing restrictions upon "black-white" out-of-wedlock unions and marriages. Although these first statutes did not prohibit marriages between "blacks" and "whites," they were designed to guarantee that the partners and children of these interracial matches would be relegated to the status of servants or slaves for many years, if not forever. During this period of colonial history, many "whites" were indentured servants, and "blacks" were laborers and servants—not yet legally defined as slaves. Marriages were not uncommon among these poor, lower class "whites" and "blacks" who worked together and occupied similar social and economic positions.[35] However, the way was being paved for children of these unions not to be able to claim their "white" origins. Legalities were being arranged to insure that the life circumstances of Negroes' mates and children would be determined by the "black" condition, soon to be chattel slavery—dehumanizing, animal-equivalent bondage.

The Maryland and Virginia laws were probably motivated more by economic than by "racial" considerations. Plantation owners were able to increase their worker numbers at little cost through these family formations. "Race" was not even a scientific concept in America at that time.

Americans today have not been told through their history courses or school books that the so-called racial classifications of people, now assumed to be important, were not even introduced in Western civilization until almost 100 years after these first miscegenation laws were enacted. It is hardly believable that the first systematic or scientific efforts to divide human beings into separate and distinct "racial" groups occurred in the mid-1700s, less than 250 years ago.[36] That these attempts to classify people into "races" did not peak until the twentieth century is more astounding. It is highly unlikely that vast numbers of U. S. citizens have given much thought to the origin of so-called racial groupings. The masses probably assume that "racial" categories were handed down from "On High," perhaps in the fashion of "The Ten Commandments."

No "racial" issue still strikes at the nerve center of American racism so piercingly as does the threat of "race-mixing." School integration remains a primary target for "race purists" who may fear forever that bringing "black" children and "white" children together in the elementary and secondary schools will lead to increased "interracial" marriages. These segregationists are fully unwilling to recognize the "white blood" which flows through millions of Americans who call themselves "black" but whose origins include "white" plantation owners, slave masters and American gentry. This "white" heritage is totally unacknowledged or repudiated by those to whom "white" means only "pure white." It is likewise unclaimed by the multitude of people who range in color from dark brown to beige to mirror-image "white" who call themselves "black."

The reality of "race-mixing" which has produced amalgamated, American progeny must be obvious, at times, to the most sheltered, unperceptive individuals. Even they must recognize the naked truth and the self-deceptive and inconsistent behaviors surrounding this issue. In his study *An American Dilemma*, the Swedish scholar Myrdal identified amalgamation as one of the touchiest spots in American life and morals.[37] "Most people, most of the time," he said, "suppress such threats to their moral integrity together with all [of] the confusion, the ambiguity and inconsistency which lurks in the basement of Man's soul."[38] As we approach the twenty-first century, Americans continue to suppress the plain truth of what centuries of "interracial" unions have begotten.

Those with mixed origins whose physical appearance allows them to choose what to call themselves, and whose numbers are unknown, appear to have but two options in the United States, a nation which clings to the doctrine of "white purity." They may choose to claim the "white" part of their heritage; if so, they are forced to "pass," to move into the day-to-day world of "pure white," where one dare not admit to any biracial lineage. To make such an admission is to abandon any claim to being "white." Their choice is, in fact, merely a different exercise of the option taken by mirror-image "whites" who choose to call themselves "black" and are thus destined to live out their decision.

The last U. S. census count of mulattoes was made in 1920.[39] Since that time, a person born of a "white" parent and a "black" parent has been expected to choose between "black" and "white." Those who elect an option, such as "Other—Specify," a category included on the 1980 census questionnaire, may be sought by the census takers, who prefer that a decision be made from the stated categories. The careful observer will note that the only color-coded racial/ethnic categories on the 1980 census questionnaire were Black and White. That the minds of Americans have been so conditioned to think in terms of "black" and "white" is a frightening tribute to the force and power of social engineering in the United States.

By eliminating the category "mulatto," the Census Bureau authorities had, in effect, cast a vote of confidence for other governmental bodies which were hard at work extending the doctrine of "white purity." "Twenty-eight states had active anti-black-white marriage statutes in 1913, Montana and Wyoming acting later," according to Joseph Washington in his book *Marriage in Black and White*.[40] There was "nationwide concern about black-white marriages . . . reflected in the rash of bills prohibiting black-white marriages proposed to state legislatures in 1913."[41]

By enacting statutes to prevent intermarriage between "blacks" and "whites," a state's lawmakers then had to define a "black" person in legal terms. This process had gained ground in those catastrophic years following Reconstruction and carried well into the twentieth century. Some Southern states passed laws which made one a "Negro" if one-sixteenth or even a known trace of "Negro-blood" could be demonstrated in the person's heritage. Other states developed similar but less stringent laws where one-fourth or one-eighth "Negro-blood" made one a Negro.[42] One could be a "Negro" in one state and a "white" in another under such conflicting statutes. William Zabel, an attorney, studied the vagaries of these definitions and concluded that they were "sometimes contradictory, often nonexistent, and usually a combination of legal fiction and genetic nonsense nearly impossible to apply as a practical matter."[43]

This powerful myth of "one black drop"—"genetic nonsense" and "legal fiction" that it is—nevertheless lingers as a syphilitic symptom in our nation's history. That educators can so readily detect "one black drop," even sorting out a "black drop" from Hispanic, Indian or Asian "drops," is a constant source of amazement for members of our family.

A person at a PTA function once referred to our daughter Monti as "a beautiful, black child." (Why not "a beautiful child?" How often does one hear a person say "a beautiful, white child?" But that's not the point here.) Like most parents, I am expected to gobble up any and all compliments and string along with these adult flatterers. There are times when I cannot do so. This was one of those times.

"Why did you call her 'black?' " I responded to this person, who was very active in school community relations.

"Well . . . she is, isn't she?" replied the person.

"Have you asked her?" I continued as politely as I could.

"No," came a faint reply, "but . . ."

I interrupted, "You do know her father . . . now you would probably call him 'white,' right?"

"Yes," said the woman in a pedantic tone, "but you do know, Mrs. Becker, that the Department of Education does say to count them black if they have one black drop in them. I know that from when I used to teach." She proceeded to explain to me how one school administrator had explained this to her.

There are teachers and school administrators, I am sure, who make the racial/ethnic headcounts without having read the U. S. Department of Education's general instructions and definitions for completing the *School System Summary Report*. Were they to do their homework, they would know that there is no mention of the "one black drop" rule in the instructions. But they do know that a child having one "black" parent and one "white" parent must be counted as either "black" or "white." Since some educators believe that when "one black drop" can be detected, they should count the child as "black," they do. Of course, "one white drop" detected in a "black" child does not taint him or her "white"!

A teacher from a southern school system told me about the year her class racial/ethnic headcount was questioned. The principal came to her classroom with the completed school headcount form she had submitted and said, "I think you've made a mistake here. You have six black children, not five." The teacher reaffirmed that she had counted five. The principal pointed to a child and said, "You see, I've heard that his father was black, and that's good enough for us." Even though this child was the mirror-image of "whiteness," a mere rumor was sufficient to satisfy the principal's headcount criteria.

On the other hand, there must be many teachers who want to and try to be supportive of children like our Monti who resists being subjected to rigid, bureaucratic instruments like the *School System Summary Report.* I once told a friend that my daughter, about to enter the fourth grade, was apparently ready to ask teachers not to count her as "black" or "white," but to count her as "biracial" when they made classroom headcounts.

"I think that's fantastic," my friend commented immediately. "You know, my brother is a teacher in a city not too far from here. He has children in his classes who are black, white, Indian, and some who are mixed. He never fills out those forms that are sent around for teachers to count children by race." My friend paused and laughed. "But when that blank form gets back to the office, the principal soon appears in my brother's classroom. The principal, a very traditional person, seems to have no problem counting heads and filling in blanks. But my brother says he won't do it. He says it isn't fair to the children."

It's a safe guess that our nation's schools are adequately staffed with teachers, principals and other administrators, unlike the above teacher, who count heads and divide children into "racial" categories without giving the process much consideration. Knowingly or unknowingly, willingly or unwillingly, the caretakers of knowledge and truth act as protectors of the doctrine of "white purity."

Ask our children where they first became aware that important, nonfamily adults will designate them as either "black" or "white" and allow no "in-betweens." They will tell you: "In school!" Often, those school officials charged with the collection of "racial/ethnic" data emphasize that the headcount categories do not denote scientific definitions or refer to biological origins. These authority figures proceed to talk about social realities—how persons are regarded by others, how individuals identify themselves. The result is, they say, a *social* definition of "race." However, data collected on this *social* basis and classified as "racial/ethnic" in a chart may quickly become "racial breakdown" or "racial balance" in the narrative explaining the statistics. The reader, uninformed about the bureaucratic *social* definitions of "race," then sees what appears to be a biological reality, given credibility through a subtle change in language. Understandably, people (including many social scientists and educational researchers) perceive the social classifications as biological ones and tend to lapse into age-old patterns of prejudice about superiority and inferiority. Thus, a kind of trickery occurs, and "racial/ethnic" social observations—already misleading—take on the aura of the scientific. Tragically, the American institution charged with the formal education of children becomes a primary agent in perpetuating the myth of separate and distinct "races."

Parents (and grandparents) must be credited with their important role, however. Many "black" parents labor diligently, sometimes painfully, to convince their children that there are rational reasons why they must say and believe that they are what they are not. Many, many more "white" parents promulgate the "they're-not-like-us" white purity theory, insisting that nonblack children be called "black."

As parents, Tom and I have come to the aid of our children on several occasions regarding their right to proclaim their own identities. We sent a letter to each child's teacher or counselor and principal in 1982 and 1983 to promote a better understanding between home and school. It is a practice we will likely continue.

# 20

## *A Letter to the Teacher*
### by Stanli and Tom

Dear   (Teacher/Counselor's name)

   Soon our child  (name of child)   will begin a new school placement under your direction. The purposes of this correspondence are: (1) to create an awareness of certain basic beliefs held by our family, and (2) to ask for your understanding when dealing with situations which we recognize as controversial to some and acknowledge as sensitive to us and our children. Our concern is personal in nature and is related to the "racial/ethnic" identity of our children and ourselves.

   The five Becker children attend four different schools in the Shaker Heights City School District. We are a so-called interracial family, residents of Shaker Heights for more than ten years. We are a family of many different skin colors, ranging from ivory to ebony, including pink, ecru, tan, honey and dark brown. Our children have

---

Note:  Permission of the authors will be granted, without charge, to an interested person or group of persons who may wish to use "A Letter to the Teacher" in whole or in part. Permission will likewise be granted to those who wish to adapt "A Letter to the Teacher" to a personal or group situation. To obtain permission, write to Seven Shadows Press, P. O. Box 1118, Cleveland, OH 44120. Enclose a self-addressed, stamped envelope with the request.

learned to recognize, accept and understand these obvious physical differences as individual characteristics, normal variations in people. This outlook has evolved quite naturally because of the composition, philosophy and lifestyle of our family. We have not simply come together as a family in the biological sense—four of our five children are adopted. However, our family "bonding" process is much like the parent-offspring model of traditional American family social structure.

As our children gain years, knowledge and understanding, they may be moved in their own ways to discuss why we—all seven of us—reject any suggestions that there are separate and distinct "races." We are quite conscious of this because of the day-to-day interactions among members of our family which demonstrate the concept of distinguishable "races," other than human, as absurd. Our children learn early in life what too few people learn later from physical anthropology: that people in modern society, with few exceptions, are visible representatives of various so-called racial/ethnic origins.

Though we alert and caution them that few others may think as they do, our children venture into the community—with school usually the first testing ground—to learn through personal experience that the color of one's skin is a serious matter to others. They meet other children and adults who, unlike them, attempt to define and rigidly divide and categorize human beings into "black" and "white."

We do teach our children that many, many people in the United States try to classify the population into *socially* defined racial/ethnic groups. For example, at the time of the census we explained to the children that item four on the census questionnaire attempted to do just that. We also pointed out to them that the Census Bureau dropped the term "race" in the 1980 census questionnaire; we discussed the reasons for this change. After considerable discussion, we, as a family, chose not to identify with a particular "racial/ethnic" group and checked the category "Other," specifying that we are "a biracial and/or multiracial family and identify ourselves as human." Our declaration is a matter of record and reflects, clearly, one of the very deep beliefs held by this family; it is a major part of the unifying philosophy that binds us together; it is a key to understanding us and our children. Given this background, one might begin to understand why our children often refer to themselves, when asked, as "biracial" or "human," or even by the actual colors of their skin. How each of our children chooses to identify himself or herself will ultimately be a matter of self-determination. We consider this to be a basic human right of every child. We will respect their choices; we ask that you also respect their choices.

During this past year, our children have been more frequently subjected to abusive racial slurs going to and returning from school, as well as on the playgrounds. We have discussed with them many pejorative terms, including "Nigger," "White Nigger," "Black Honky," "Oreo" and "Zebra," the last two being directed at children who have one "black" parent and one "white" parent. Children, like adults, usually react when offended or hurt. As one might expect, our children will respond to these affronts, sometimes appropriately, sometimes inappropriately.

We work diligently with our children in the hope that each will learn to cope with so-called racial conflicts in socially acceptable ways. However, we do encourage them to maintain their own beliefs and to think for themselves. We trust that this letter will be helpful to you in better understanding us and our children in whatever related situations may arise in the school setting.

Sincerely,

Stanli K. Becker<br>
John T. Becker

# 21

## *What Natural Parting*
by Tom

"It's natural to seek your own kind." So said an adult to the panel of senior high school students and the forty or more persons crowded into one of Shaker High's classrooms. Three or four other people nodded in agreement. This workshop was one of several offered at the second meeting of a two-part program addressing interracial relations in Ohio's Shaker Heights schools.

The teenage panelists were poised, articulate and coolheaded as they interacted among themselves and with those in the audience before them. One student talked about the more positive atmosphere at Shaker High than at some of the other area suburban high schools. No one on the panel vehemently disagreed with him. Another student, however, did admit to the existence of separation and alienation between "black" students and "white" students. She referred to the fourth grade as a point where changing attitudes about "black" and "white" had become more noticeable among her friends and classmates. Several other panelists appeared to agree.

Eight weeks had passed since Stanli and I had attended the first of the two meetings. What drew our attention to the first meeting was the advance publicity flyer sent to parents. The theme was boldly presented as "ALIENS AND ALLIES: a description of student interracial relations in the Shaker Schools." This one page flyer was divided into two diagonally placed white quarters in juxtaposition with two diagonally placed black quarters. White letters were contrasted against the black background and black letters against the white. An outline of a face was placed in the center: a white eye on black, a black eye on white; a half nose and a half mouth appeared on the white background, but the other halves of the nose and mouth were conspicuously absent on the black background. The impression was that the black face was incomplete. Stanli and I weren't the only ones to notice this difference.

About midway through this first public forum, a man in the auditorium arose to express his annoyance at the design of this sharply contrasted black and white flyer. He inquired about the dubious title "ALIENS AND ALLIES." He raised the poignant question about who should assume the role of "ALIENS"? Were blacks being led to think that they were the "ALIENS"? Were whites to think that they were the "ALLIES"? Just what was the status of blacks in the nationally-known, integrated, suburban community of Shaker Heights?

Numerous examples of "racial" division and alienation sallied forth from people in attendance that evening. In school sports, there were the mostly "white" hockey team and the mostly "black" basketball team. The high school majorette corps was described as "solid black." At the high school in the levels system (a practice of grouping students based on presumed academic ability and past performance), a disproportionate and large number of "black" students were said to be in the lower levels.

The existence of some "all-white" dances and some "all-black" dances surfaced; these social occasions were readily explained by those articulating the theory of natural attraction. They espouse, among other things, that "blacks" suddenly become interested only in "blacks" with the onset of teenage sex urges. It follows, so say the disciples of natural attraction, that "whites" come to realize that they are attracted to "whites" only. At least this kind of thinking is a far cry from that of a judge who, in an old Missouri case, proclaimed that "blacks" and "whites" were biologically unable to produce fertile offspring.[44] He offered this explanation in justifying those laws which prohibited intermarriage between "blacks" and "whites." How pleasing such preposterous judgments must have been to those extremists in America at that time who preached that horses don't mix with cows, dogs don't mix with hogs and "blacks" don't mix with "whites." These are still welcome words to the ears of present-day, die-hard segregationists.

One "black" mother at the meeting described how her daughter was invited to visit a "white" friend's house; however, the "white" friend was forbidden to come to visit her "black" friend's house. The message is clear in these kinds of situations: the natural desires of children are being thwarted by parental design. Our family's experiences and observations lead me to believe that these people may constitute a minority in the integrated community of Shaker Heights.

There are many concerned citizens in Shaker Heights who, like those participants in the "ALIENS AND ALLIES" affair, recognize problems and work painstakingly to resolve them. The city maintains a Housing Office which encourages "white" families to buy or rent in "substantially integrated areas." What that means is that a lot of "blacks" live in those areas. The Housing Office will also assist "black" families to buy or rent in areas of this suburban city which have a "lesser degree of integration." That means mostly "white." Prospective new families with the financial resources truly have a choice as to whether they want their child or children to attend neighborhood schools with other children who are said to be "different." This effort at grassroots integration has had its share of successes, but it has not halted the development of predominantly "black" residential zones.

Therefore, the Board of Education is necessarily an integral part of the Shaker Heights integration blueprint. Its response to neighborhood schools which have failed to produce a statistically satisfactory variety of skin colors is "voluntary busing." The Shaker Schools Plan is an attempt to achieve "racial balance" in the twelve schools of this district. At present, this voluntary busing endeavor—not to be confused with "forced busing"—is tied into a magnet school-type program on the elementary level called Choices for Children. CHOICES stands for Campaign to Help Obtain Integration and Challenging Education in Shaker. The CHOICES program has created opportunities for children in the elementary schools to enroll in four major offerings—Program for the Gifted, Computer Education, Science and French. These elementary schools are often called "Mini-Magnets" because the CHOICES program does not convert them into total magnet schools. The children accepted into the CHOICES offerings at a particular school also follow the regular curriculum of that school. But, as with all promotions and enticements, there's a catch: those children who, by accident of the color of their skin, can help the schools achieve "racial balance" are the ones accepted into the special programs of CHOICES. For example, children of majority-culture-skin-colors will be accepted for a special program in an elementary school of high minority enrollment. Conversely, brown-skinned minority children are candidates for enrollment in the predominately "white" schools which offer special opportunities under CHOICES.

The housing and busing programs have received some national acclaim. Many of the people who created, backed, or stood behind these programs deserve much more than just a good pat on the back for their efforts and the headway which has been made. The city government and the Board of Education, cooperating as they do in these school and housing integration efforts, may be far ahead of many other suburban communities throughout the nation.

In 1979, the year in which the programs addressing interracial relations in the Shaker Heights schools took place, renewed "racial" polarization had become a fact of life in the United States. Many citizens who had once cried "Keep the faith, baby!" had lost the faith. Vocal "blacks," who felt robbed of their gains in the 1960s, talked about "the man" or the "theys" or "them downtown" or "them in Washington" who never wanted to open the doors to "blacks" in the first place. Noted writer, historian and senior editor of *Ebony* magazine, Lerone Bennett, Jr., compared the late 1970s to those of the late 1870s, just prior to the decades in which "the first Reconstruction ended in a major historical catastrophe that wiped out the gains of the 1860s."[45]

Vocal "whites," who felt they'd already given up too much, asked, "What more do they want?" In increasing numbers, "whites" focused their attention on jobs, reverse discrimination, good schools and efforts to snatch children from the jaws of "forced busing" which had fallen on bad times. Congress had debated proposals to end it; recent presidents had spoken out against it. Radio, TV and the press had given extensive coverage to antibusing developments in major urban areas, and people—both "black" and "white"—questioned whether it was "worth all the trouble." There were many outspoken critics of "forced busing," but there was one, in particular, who caught the attention of the news media.

On June 5, 1975, a front-page article appeared in *The National Observer* entitled "A Scholar Who Inspired It Says . . . Busing Backfired."[46] The title led me to think that some scholar had decided to "eat crow" about his own work. That had reader appeal, especially to the foes of "forced busing" who had little use for the scholars who inspired it or the judges who ordered it. But the best was yet to come. The article introduced a man who could oppose "forced busing" and at the same time speak out in favor of racial intermarriage.

This highly regarded scholar Dr. James S. Coleman, then professor of sociology at the University of Chicago, had gained national prominence in 1966 as the senior author of *Equality of Educational Opportunity*, a report to the then existing Office of Health, Education, and Welfare. This study implied that "black" children in integrated classrooms would achieve more than if they were in segregated classrooms. The "Coleman Report" was used to support school desegregation efforts in the late 1960s and early 1970s, including desegregation through busing. Coleman, however, thought that the courts were wrong to use his report as the rationale for these rulings. He had never intended to inspire court-ordered busing as a means of achieving integration in the schools.

In the mid-1970s, he became quite blunt in interviews about his opposition to court-ordered desegregation plans, such as "forced busing." Coleman commented frankly on issues like "white flight," the "high degree of disorder" in "lower-class black classrooms," and racial intermarriage. All of this made for bigger and more stirring news. Even Coleman's critics acknowledged that his opinions were sought and written about by editors and reporters on a scale remarkable for a sociologist.

In *The National Observer* interview, the Coleman appeal was undoubtedly magnified by his frank advocacy of racial intermarriage. He said: ". . . school desegregation is not the only way to promote social integration. Nor is it, I believe, the best way. For example, activities that encourage racial intermarriage could be much more effective in creating stable forces for social integration."[47] A short time thereafter, Dr. Coleman was invited to be a major participant at a consultation sponsored by the U.S. Commission on Civil Rights on the issue of school desegregation and suburban migration (often called "white flight"). Once again the subject of racial intermarriage surfaced. Coleman elaborated on his views. He was critical of "well-intentioned white liberals" and their efforts to bring about integration in the schools and society. He said:

> I think it is extremely important to have a reasonably large set of interested parties in the sense that their interests are very fundamental, at the very level of the home, parties interested in the very integration of society. . . . I am not saying racial intermarriage is going to be an immediate and overwhelming thing. What I am saying is it should be encouraged precisely for that reason, precisely because of the fact that it creates a set of interested parties whose orientation to this issue is not so fragile as that of a set of white liberals who happen to live in the suburbs.[48]

Indeed, there had been a large-scale defection of "white" liberals from the cause at the time Coleman expressed his opinions. No doubt, some were the same, well-intentioned, but fragile, "white" liberals of whom he spoke. They may even have been among the outspoken in the 1960s—those who worked diligently at getting borderline and hard-core bigots to experiment with personal change in those hope-filled, idealistic years.

"Come to our encounter group" could have been the invitation to join others who were examining and analyzing their attitudes and behaviors in newly-popularized ways. The encounter group, in which "blacks" and "whites" met together, very often gathered in a volunteer's living room. Through existing good will, people believed that they could face problems squarely and do something to solve them, starting at their own front doors, if you will.

More formal encounter groups were sponsored by religious and community organizations and emerging, sensitivity training centers. Encounter groups consisted of eight to twenty persons who willingly came together to experience things. Leaders introduced various games which were played in these meetings, such as pretending that a "black" family was moving into a "white" neighborhood. "Whites" were asked to pretend to be "black" and "blacks" to be "white." They became actors and actresses who carried out the pretend activities; then, the group talked about what the actors and actresses did in these circumstances. The more daring group leaders introduced activities such as having a "white" participant and a "black" participant stare into each other's eyes until one of them expressed a feeling of anger or affection. The individuals then discussed these feelings and emotions. The goal was to increase understanding and broaden thinking.

Caught up in these encounter groups and the romanticism of the Civil Rights Movement, some "white" neighborhoods formed groups to plan for and support integration in their communities. Based on the mutual support they got from each other through these group-engaging activities, they were willing to take some risks, like planning how to welcome a "black" family. What they were not prepared for was meaningful integration. That any family—not just one or two—having the means and the desire to live in the neighborhood of its choice might become a reality, the norm, was never really seriously considered by many of the "white" supporters and activists.

The number of "blacks" with the economic status to seek out the Great American Dream gradually multiplied in the 1950s and increased further in the 1960s. They moved out of the central city areas into the suburbs in great numbers. This urban exodus did not go undetected; it was definitely not in the game plan. In time, many of the same "white" liberals, who had once said, "Some of my best friends are Negroes," could be heard saying, "Damn it! Can you believe it? Some more of them moved into the neighborhood last week."

Many of those who resisted block-busting in the 1960s because of their beliefs seemingly became overwhelmed by numbers. That more than one black per block or so might cause property values to drop was one new fear. It was no secret either that there had been an upsurge in "interracial" dating and marriages during these years of the encounter groups and civil rights activities. That well-known persons of distinction, Dr. Coleman, for example, would give encouragement publicly to "interracial" couples was a new twist. Now the insecure "white" liberal had to grapple with the thought that the "natural parting" might not, after all, be based on truth.

The attempt to disperse and divide children or adults because of skin color or some other easily noted features remains today as one of the most heartless legacies of the long history of "white racism" in America. Racism feeds upon the practice of violating natural associations and feelings. The Missouri judge who would deny marriage to "interracial" couples because of his belief that they could not produce fertile offspring was himself interfering with the natural order of things. The same can be said for any "white" parent who forbids his or her child to visit a "black" friend's home because of prejudiced views about people of different skin coloration. There is no evidence of a natural parting in the lives of our children; we believe that to be true of all children. When parting does occur among young boys and girls of different skin colors in the fourth grade or junior high or senior high—and it does—it is because it has been learned. Such parting is taught in the home, the school, the community and the nation. It is a learned parting, not a natural parting; it is, as J. A. Rogers might have put it, "the result of certain ignorant teachings."[49]

In 1970, a Joint Commission on Mental Health in Children stated that "racism is the number one public health problem facing America today."[50] It will remain so until we free children from the oppressive, man-made artificiality of race-thinking" which strives to cloud and obscure the universality of humanness.

# 22

## *Why Bus Me*
### by Monti

When I was in the second grade, a picture of a friend and me together appeared in the *Shaker Heights School Review* with the caption: "Bus Routes to Friendships: The Enlarged Shaker Schools Plan."[51] Mom and Dad had no idea that this picture had been taken or that it was going to be published in the *School Review*. I was really surprised when Mom and Dad showed me the picture, because neither my friend nor I was bused to school.

It sounds funny now, but I remember counting the steps on the route from school to my friend's house and then from school to mine. I lived 42 steps closer to school than she, and I thought that my friend was going to be bused because she lived farther away. When I told Mom about my house-to-school counting, she stared at me with a puzzled look on her face; then suddenly she flung her head and folded arms onto the kitchen counter and burst out laughing. She laughed until tears were in her eyes. "Just wait until your father hears that," Mom said with a big grin and a few more chuckles. "He'll crack up, too!"

I didn't know that my friend and I were looked upon as children of different "races" when I first saw the picture. I thought busing was for those kids who lived farthest away from school.

Really, I couldn't have been bused at that time. It

would have been against the busing rules. To be bused to my elementary school, Onaway, a child not only had to be "black" or minority, but also had to live in one of three certain school neighborhoods farther away than my own. And where did I live? Around the corner—about a five or ten minute walk from Onaway. Some people in the school system didn't do their homework!

What makes the whole thing funnier is that my neighbor and I didn't become friends through "bus routes," like the caption read. We were playmates long before then. That's because we lived so close together.

It's easy to laugh at mix-ups like the picture in the *School Review*. However, there are times when it's hard for me to laugh. Those "racial/ethnic" headcounts turn me off when the teachers work on them during my classes. I especially don't like it when these counts are conducted openly in the classroom before my friends and classmates. It's hard on me because there are only five choices, and none of them fits me. I don't like to make a choice between "black" and "white" because I am both! That's like trying to make me choose between my dad and mom—and in front of everyone else, too!

It just doesn't make sense for judges, lawyers, parents and teachers to bus kids, integrate schools and classes, and then turn around and say that there can't be any integrated kids.

The kids I go to school with know that there are integrated people! Take those guys who try to give me a hard time, or even my friends when they're teasing or being mean or trying to "play crazy." I especially remember one day in sixth grade when a friend and I were walking home from school. My friend was also from an "interracial" family. Some boys across the street yelled to us, "Hey, Zebras!" "Zebra" is supposed to mean that you have one "white" parent and one "black" parent. We just yelled back, "Yeah, and we're proud of it!" Most of the time, boys who tease us just laugh, jump around pointing at us, yell "Zebra" a few more times, and then if we ignore them, they get bored and go away. Dad says that the boys are just teasing or flirting with us. Anyway, nothing serious seems to come from that kind of stuff, except we might feel "funny" or have our feelings hurt for a little while.

It's not a big thing to my friends. I think they respect me and my family for sticking to what we believe. A couple of years ago, one of my friends joked about me and the other kids in my class: "This year in our room we've got a perfect split—9½ blacks and 9½ whites." Everyone who heard that and knew me cracked up.

# 23

## *To Kill a Myth*
### by Stanli and Tom

*The American Heritage Dictionary of the English Language* defines a myth as "a notion based more on tradition or convenience than on fact."[52] Facts, when known, reveal myths for the falsehoods that they are.

Americans, in the main, are not exposed to the facts about "race." In school, children read from social studies textbooks which are sometimes ten, twenty or more years old. These outdated learning tools still refer to the traditional "three races of mankind." They treat the concept of "race" in too few, vague, simplistic paragraphs which are often inexact, incomplete or misleading in view of what is known and accepted today in anthropology. Teachers and school administrators classify children according to "race," sometimes secretively, furtively, and other times openly in the classroom. School bulletins and annual reports feed the results of these headcounts to communities in the form of the U.S. Department of Education's rigid, five-category, racial/ethnic *School System Summary Report*, an instrument which denies children the right to claim more than one part of their ancestry. At home, both children and adults are bombarded daily by news coverage, specials and other TV programs which reinforce the notions of a "black race" and a "white race." In these ways, the myth of separate and distinct races is perpetuated and woven into the social, economic, political and religious fabrics of our nation; facts become obscured; convenience and custom rule the day.

We, as a people, continue to ignore the words and admonitions of those respected scholars who have argued convincingly that race is "superstition," "myth," "modern witchcraft."[53] Their scientific findings and scholarly judgments appear to fall by the wayside and have little, if any, impact on the beliefs and day-to-day, practical life experiences of common men and women. The sober truth is that most people willingly identify themselves by "race." Many of them do so without giving much thought to the process. Thus, they meet a societal expectation—one with a very long tradition.

Our parents, grandparents and those before them identified themselves, or were identified by others, as "colored, Negro, black" or "Caucasian, white." We followed the same practice, even into the early years of our marriage. That we have chosen to change this pattern has been, in great part, the subject of this book.

We have almost no measure of how many "interracial" families share similar feelings about this issue. However, we recognize that it is precisely because of our blending, what most would call our interracial living experience, that we have reviewed, reconsidered and revised our thinking. We conducted research on the facts about "race"; we gained information new to us; we reshaped our attitudes—and actions—in accordance. We are alike in too many significant ways to continue to believe or act as if differences in skin color, hair texture or other discernible features, often minor in comparison, can be lumped together to divide us, even through the creation of awesome-sounding "races."

In our protective family environment, we view "race" as the absurdity that it is, focusing our attention instead on matters that truly influence the quality of life and the deepening development of personhood, humanness. To kill the myth of race in the safety and security of the sheltered family unit is, however, quite a different challenge than to assault the same in the expanded social groups of neighborhood, community, city and state. We carefully teach our children not to delude themselves into thinking that they—or we alone—can change the ways, customs or traditions of our racially-divided society. But we strongly encourage them to maintain their own thinking and to look for like thinkers, other people who have similar beliefs. As the opportunities to do so arise, we give them examples of individuals and groups working in the same vein.

Our purpose in writing this book is not to propose grand solutions designed to unseat this deep-rooted notion of "race" from the social and political institutions which preserve and perpetuate it. We are aware of ways in which we ourselves succumb to the semantics and concept of "race." We have done so continually throughout this book, even though we attempt to avoid the trap by setting off in quotation marks words like "black," "white," "biracial" and "interracial." In this respect, we are guilty of what we criticize!

It seems there are numbers of other people in the U.S. who could step forward, expose "race" for the absurdity it is and refuse to continue kowtowing to the things that accompany it. They don't—often, for reasons too numerous to list in their entirety. Commonly, some choose not to cause ripples, others are too busy with the practical adjustments required for social and economic self-preservation. Certainly, seeking jobs, protecting one's position, meeting mortgage and car payments, raising children, pursuing recreation and more prove taxing and consuming. Besides, why make life's adaptations and problems more difficult than they are already?

Once in a while, our children do meet or learn of important adults who step forward to challenge the idea of separate and distinct races. In 1980, at age ten, Monti received a letter and a news clipping from her great-aunt Sister Helen, a Catholic nun. The title of the article was "White? Black? Yellow? Other?" It appeared in a statewide publication of the Ohio Province of the Sisters of Notre Dame.[54] The article described how a small Catholic elementary school had amended the choices under racial classifications on its registration forms. For example, a child of a "black" parent and a "white" parent could now declare himself or herself "biracial," as could children of other so-called interracial unions.

The report went on to describe a ten-year-old girl who chose not to identify as "black" or "white"—a child with "a strong sense of self-worth and security" who saw herself as being both "black" and "white," but not one to the exclusion of the other. "This child of ten is her own person," wrote the reporter, who then attributed several quotations to the young biracial child. Monti quickly recognized herself as the girl being discussed, as did we.

"I said all that?" squealed Monti, a big smile breaking. The story concluded by suggesting that Monti and other children of nontraditional interracial unions "who think as she does" represent a "Fourth World, perhaps—right in our own midst."

Later, Aunt Helen confessed in her usual, warm, humorous manner that she had been at the bottom of this "cause." The principal was both a friend and colleague of hers. She told us how that principal had come to know Monti through family photographs and, of course, Aunt Helen's descriptions of our family's lifestyle.

We applaud the courage of the principal of that small Catholic elementary school in Dayton, Ohio; school administrators in both public and private schools ought to take note of her actions. We think she was right in collecting the "racial/ethnic" data as she did. The 1978 Federal Register Directive, referred to earlier, states clearly that "in no case should the provisions of this Directive be construed to limit the collection of data to the categories described above."[55] (The categories here referred to are (1) American Indian or Alaskan Native, (2) Asian or Pacific Islander, (3) Black, not of Hispanic origin, (4) Hispanic, (5) White, not of Hispanic origin.) What the 1978 Directive does require is that the methods employed in collecting "racial/ethnic" data, however detailed, be organized and "aggregated" into the above categories for purposes of federal statistics and program reporting. A safe guess is that few teachers and principals realize that the actual classroom "racial/ethnic" headcounts need not be limited to the above categories, for they are not so apprised in the instructions of the *School System Summary Report* issued by the U.S. Department of Education. Were educators so informed, there are surely others, like the principal above, who would not collect data which ignore "biracialness," particularly when these headcounts take place openly in the classroom with classifications announced and noses assigned to them. There are teachers and principals, we know, who want to respect all of a child's origins. The humanist-oriented classroom is a proper environment in which to do so. One alternative might be to "pass the buck" back to the bureaucrats. A teacher or principal could collect "racial/ethnic" data in a way which would respect children's chosen identities—and their feelings! Then let the administrators "aggregate" this data for the U.S. Department of Education. Still better, have parents write the racial/ethnic designation appropriate for them and their children on any given form that the system may require.

How each of our children chooses to identify himself or herself will ultimately be a matter of self-determination. We consider this to be a basic human right. As parents, we will respect their choices. We cannot promise our children that others will do likewise.

# *Epilogue*
## by Stanli

"I'm sorry you can't get married at First Baptist. Stanli ought to be able to get married in the church where she grew up." My mother's eyes watered as she talked to Tom, handing him a wedding gift. He and I were leaving Charleston for New York City to marry before a yet unselected justice of the peace. It was *illegal* for a "black" person to wed a "white" person in West Virginia, one of 17 states still having antimiscegenation laws in 1967. The issue was already before the United States Supreme Court; we did not wish to wait for the ruling.

It is probably true that every couple in any of the fifty states entering a so-called interracial marriage does so with serious contemplation. Whether "love will prevail" or other forces conquer will be part of that pondering. Various people, including family, friends, colleagues and acquaintances—some well-intentioned and some not—prove more than willing to advise: "Think of all the problems you'll have." "What about your careers?" "Where will you live?" "What about your children?"

Tom and I decided to marry, well aware of the "black" and "white" crosscurrents of criticism we would face. National polls at that time showed that the majority of Americans professed disapproval of "black-white" marriages. Many people dismissed "interracial" couples as dreamers in quest of unreachable goals, people "bucking the system" and falling outside of it. The nation's moviegoers had to wait until the late 1960s to view the movie, "Guess Who's Coming to Dinner?" This film about the courtship and marriage of a "black" man and a "white" woman starred several of Hollywood's most notables—Katherine Hepburn, Spencer Tracy and Sidney Poitier. The marriage of the daughter of President Johnson's Secretary of State to a "black" man made national news. These were the occurrences of yesterdays and yesteryears.

Any number of the barriers, difficulties and attitudes Tom and I have encountered in the past are still present in some form. Notwithstanding, we have always found comfortable living accommodations, and our careers have not been hindered because of our "black-white" marriage. In those few instances when we have suffered vicious verbal and physical abuse, we are not unlike many other American families. We live in a violent society, and people of all colors and backgrounds are numbered among its victims for a wide variety of reasons.

In 1984, our children can watch "Different Strokes" and "Webster" on television. As much as they like these popular TV series, they also easily detect the missing components. They have observed aloud that the important, parental models for TV's prime time "black" children, Arnold and Webster, are all "white"; and, our children have asked, "Why?" They have noted, too, that they see no families similar to ours on "the tube" or in the movies, while they see many other families resembling ours in Shaker Heights and at the shopping malls. The only regularly seen "black-white" TV couple are Helen and Tom, friends of George and Louise on "The Jeffersons." The low-profile of "black-white" family life on television reminds one of the near invisibility of minorities in the early days of TV. The media reinforces the fear of the masses by providing no realistic outlet for the situations of "black-white" families which number easily in the hundreds of thousands, perhaps in numbers greater than known to those who collect statistics.

In sixteen years, the year 2000, our children will reach the ages of 30, 28, 27, 25 and 24. No one can say with certainty what lifestyles will endure into the twenty-first century. The opportunities for achieving true humanness in civilization reside in a time to come.

# *Notes*

**Preface**
1. Ashley Montagu, *Man's Most Dangerous Myth: the Fallacy of Race* (New York: Oxford University Press, 1974), p. 3.
2. Jacques Barzun, *Race: a Study in Superstition*, revised (New York: Harper & Row, Publishers, 1965). The first edition was published in 1937, entitled *Race: a Study in Modern Superstition.*

**One Black Drop**
3. Langston Hughes, *Simple Takes a Wife* (New York: Simon and Schuster, 1953), p. 85.

**Reductio Ad Absurdum**
4. Gunner Myrdal, *An American Dilemma: the Negro Problem & Modern Democracy*, Vol. I (New York: Pantheon Books, Division of Random House, 1962), p. 58. Reprint of 20th anniversary edition published by Harper & Row.
5. See A. Leon Higginbotham, Jr., *In the Matter of Color: Race and the American Legal Process: the Colonial Period* (New York: Oxford University Press, 1978), pp. 41-42; William D. Zabel, "Interracial Marriage and the Law," *Atlantic Monthly*, Vol. 216, No. 4 (October, 1965), pp. 75-76; Robert J. Sickels, *Race, Marriage and the Law* (Alburquerque: University of New Mexico Press, 1972), pp. 3-7.
6. See Ernest Porterfield, *Black and White Mixed Marriages: an Ethnographic Study of Black-White Families* (Chicago: Nelson-Hall, Inc., 1978), pp. 4-6; Joseph R. Washington, Jr., *Marriage in Black and White* (Boston:

Beacon Press, 1970), pp. 98-148; Joel Williamson, *New People: Miscegenation and Mulattoes in the United States* (New York: The Free Press, 1980), pp. 100-109; Robert S. Stuckert, "The African Ancestry of the White American Population," Vol. 58, No. 3 *Ohio Journal of Science*, (May, 1958), pp. 155-160; J. A. Rogers, *Nature Knows No Color-Line*, 3rd ed. (Helga M. Rogers, 1270 Fifth Avenue, New York, N.Y. 10029, 1952), pp. 191-203.

7. Poppy Cannon, *A Gentle Knight: My Husband, Walter White* (New York, N.Y.: Rinehart and Company, Inc., 1956).
8. Cannon, p. 14.
9. Walter White, *A Man Called White* (New York: Arno Press & The New York Times, 1969).
10. White, pp. 363-64.
11. This quotation first appeared in Walter White, "Why I Remain a Negro," *Saturday Review of Literature*, Vol. XXX, No. 41 (October 11, 1947), p. 13; later, it appeared in his autobiography, *A Man Called White*.
12. Cannon, p. 18.
13. Ridgely Torrence, *The Story of John Hope* (New York: Arno Press & The New York Times, 1969).
14. An editorial by W. E. B. DuBois from the *Pittsburgh Courier*, March 28, 1936, as quoted by Torrence, p. 375.
15. Torrence, pp. 149-50.
16. Torrence, p. 151.
17. An editorial by W. E. B. DuBois from the *Pittsburgh Courier*, March 28, 1936, as quoted by Torrence, p. 375.

**Race-Thinking**

18. Barzun, p. ix.
19. J. A. Rogers, *From "Superman" to Man*, 5th ed. Reprinted in 1982 (Helga M. Rogers, 1270 Fifth Avenue, New York, N.Y. 10029, 1968).
20. Rogers, *From "Superman" to Man*, p. 130.
21. J. A. Rogers, *100 Amazing Facts about the Negro with Complete Proof* (Helga M. Rogers, 1270 Fifth Avenue, New York, N.Y. 10029, 1970 edition).
22. J. A. Rogers, *Nature Knows No Color-Line: Research into the Negro Ancestry in the White Race*, 3rd ed. (Helga M. Rogers, 1270 Fifth Avenue, New York, N.Y.

10029, 1952); and *Sex and Race: a History of White, Negro, and Indian Miscegenation in the Two Americas*, 3 vols. (Helga M. Rogers, 1270 Fifth Avenue, New York, N.Y. 10029). The editions of *Sex and Race* referred to are: Volume I, ninth edition, 1967; Volume II, copyright 1942, renewed 1970; Volume III, copyright 1944, renewed 1972.

23. Rogers, *Sex and Race*, Vol. II, Foreward.
24. Rogers, *Nature Knows No Color-Line*, p. 2.

**Blackness and Reality**

25. Bertha Rogers, *Little Brown Baby: Paul Laurence Dunbar, Poems for Young People; Selections, with Biographical Sketch*. Illustrated by Erick Berry (New York: Dodd, Mead & Company, 1968).
26. Paul R. Ehrlich and S. Shirley Feldman, *The Race Bomb: Skin Color, Prejudice, and Intelligence* (New York: Ballantine Books, 1977), pp. 1–2.
27. Gwendolyn Brooks, *Primer for Blacks* (The Black Position Press, 7428 South Evans Avenue, Chicago, Illinois 60619, 1980).
28. Brooks, p. 14.

**They Don't Count Me**

29. *The Schools of Shaker Heights: everyone a winner!* 1980–81 Annual Report of the Shaker Heights City School District, Shaker Heights, Ohio 44120.

**Mixed Origins**

30. *School System Summary Report: Form AS/CR 101*, Definitions, Office for Civil Rights, U.S. Department of Education, Washington, D.C. 20202.
31. School System Summary Report, Definitions.
32. School System Summary Report, Definitions.
33. School System Summary Report, Definitions.
34. Directive 15, *Federal Register*, Vol. 43, No. 87—Thursday, May 4, 1978, p. 19269.
35. See Joseph R. Washington, Jr., *Marriage in Black and White* (Boston: Beacon Press, 1970), pp. 42–44; Joel Williamson, *New People: Miscegenation and Mulattoes in the United States* (New York: The Free Press, 1980), pp. 6–10; A. Leon Higginbotham, Jr., *In the Matter of Color: Race and the American Legal Process: the Colon-*

*ial Period* (New York: Oxford University Press, 1978), pp. 20-22; J. A. Rogers, *Africa's Gift to America: the Afro-American in the Making and Saving of the United States.* Revised & enlarged Civil War Centennial Edition (Helga M. Rogers, 1270 Fifth Avenue, New York, N.Y. 10029, 1961), pp. 58-70. J. A. Rogers, *Sex and Race: a History of White, Negro and Indian Miscegenation in the Two Americas*, Vol. II (Helga M. Rogers, 1270 Fifth Avenue, New York, N.Y. 10029, 1942), pp. 155-162.

36. Paul R. Ehrlich and S. Shirley Feldman, *The Race Bomb: Skin Color, Prejudice, and Intelligence*, pp. 13-40.
37. Myrdal, *An American Dilemma*, Vol. II, p. 592.
38. Myrdal, Vol. I, p. lxvii.
39. Henry S. Shryock, Jacob S. Siegel and Associates. *The Methods and Materials of Demography.* 4th printing (rev.), Elizabeth A. Larman, Editorial Associate. U.S. Department of Commerce, June, 1980, Vol. I, p. 256.
40. Washington, *Marriage in Black and White*, p. 74.
41. Washington, p. 74.
42. William D. Zabel, "Interracial Marriage and the Law," *Atlantic Monthly*, Vol. 216, No. 4 (October, 1965) pp. 75-79; also see Washington, *Marriage in Black and White*, pp. 69-97; Williamson, *New People: Miscegenation and Mulattoes in the United States*, pp. 91-100.
43. Zabel, "Interracial Marriage and the Law," p. 77.

**What Natural Parting**

44. Robert J. Sickels, *Race, Marriage, and the Law* (Albuquerque: University of New Mexico Press, 1972), p. 99.
45. Lerone Bennett, Jr., "The Second Time Around: Will History Repeat Itself and Rob Blacks of the Gains of the 1960s?" *Ebony*, Vol. XXXVI, No. 12 (October, 1981), p. 33.
46. "A Scholar Who Inspired It Says . . . Busing Backfired." *The National Observer*, June 7, 1975, pp. 1, 18.
47. "A Scholar Who Inspired It Says . . . Busing Backfired," p. 18.
48. James S. Coleman, "School Desegregation and Loss of Whites from Large Central-City School Districts," in *School Desegregation: the Courts and Suburban Migration*. A Consultation Sponsored by the U.S. Commis-

sion on Civil Rights, Washington, D.C. 20425, December 8, 1975, p. 179.
49. Rogers, *From "Superman" to Man*, p. 130.
50. *Crisis in Child Mental Health: Challenge for the 1970s.* Report of the Joint Commission on Mental Health in Children (New York: Harper & Row, 1970), p. 216.

**Why Bus Me**
51. *Shaker Heights School Review*, No. 162, Shaker Heights, Ohio, March, 1977, p. 4.

**To Kill a Myth**
52. William Morris, Editor, *The American Heritage Dictionary of the English Language* (Boston: American Heritage Publishing Co., Inc. and Houghton Mifflin Company, 1971), p. 869.
53. See Ashley Montagu, *Man's Most Dangerous Myth: the Fallacy of Race*; Jacques Barzun, *Race: a Study in Superstition*; Paul R. Ehrlich and S. Shirley Feldman, *The Race Bomb: Skin Color, Prejudice, and Intelligence.*
54. "Speak Up," *News and Views—The Notre Dame Letter*, Ohio Province, Vol. X, No. 20, October 16, 1980.
55. Directive 15, *Federal Register*, Vol. 43, No. 87—Thursday, May 4, 1978, p. 19269.

# Index

Adoption, x, 11, 17-20, 118
Amalgamation, 44, 110; see also miscegenation and race-mixing
*American Dilemma: the Negro Problem and Modern Democracy, An* (Myrdal), 44, 110
Antimiscegenation statutes, 44, 112, 141
Atlanta University, 50

Barzun, Jacques, xi, 55
Bennett, Lerone, 125
Biracial, 53-54, 94-95, 100-102, 104-105, 111, 114, 119, 137, 138
Black culture, 78-81, 82
Black, definition of, 13, 108-112
*Black Reconstruction in America* (DuBois), 79
Brooks, Gwendolyn, 80, 82-83

Cannon, Poppy, 46-47
Caucasian, *see* white
Census (1790), 100
Census (1920), 100, 111
Census (1980), 82, 85-86, 89, 91-98, 99, 102, 104, 105, 107, 111, 118

Civil Rights Movement, 6, 12, 128-129
Coleman, James, 126-127, 129
Coleman Report, 126

"Different Strokes," 142
DuBois, W. E. B., 12, 50-51, 79
Dunbar, Paul Laurence, 12, 80

Ehrlich, Paul, 82
Encounter groups, 127-128

Federal Register Directive 15 (1978), 108, 138-139
Feldman, S. Shirley, 82
Forced busing, 124-126
*From "Superman" to Man* (Rogers), 59

*Gentle Knight: My Husband, Walter White, A* (Cannon), 46

Hope, Edward (son of John Hope), 47-51, 87
Hope, John, 47-52
Hope, Marion Conover, 87-89
Hughes, Langston, 9-10, 12, 80
Interracial families, 11, 38, 49, 65-68, 81, 95, 98, 109-110,

117–119, 132, 136–137, 141–142
Interracial marriage, 43–44, 67, 109–112, 123, 126–129, 141–143

"Jeffersons, The," 142
Joint Commission on Mental Health in Children (1970), 130

Majority-skin-color culture, 44, 50, 78, 85, 124
Malcolm X, 33, 80
*Man Called White, A* (White), 46
*Marriage in Black and White* (Washington), 112
Mayor of Cleveland's 1980 Complete Count Executive Committee, 91, 95–97, 100, 102
Mirror image, 5, 37–40, 43, 45, 52, 76, 111, 114
Miscegenation, 44, 109–111; see also amalgamation and race-mixing
Missouri judge, 123, 129
Montagu, Ashley, x
Morehouse College, 48, 51
Mulatto, 11, 85, 100–101, 111
Myrdal, Gunner, 43, 110
Myth, definition of, 135
Myth, racial, x, 75, 80, 82, 135–139

*Nature Knows No Color-Line* (Rogers), 60
Negro, *see* black
*News and Views—The Notre Dame Letter* (Ohio Province), 138

Niagara Movement, The, 50–51

One black drop, 9–14, 78, 112–113
*100 Amazing Facts about the Negro with Complete Proof* (Rogers), 59–60

Passing, 45–46, 111
*Primer for Blacks* (Brooks), 82

Race, scientific origins of, 107–110
Race, social definition of, 115, 118
Race-mixing, 44, 60, 110; *see also* amalgamation *and* miscegenation
Race-thinking, xi, 3, 55–60, 77, 82
*Race Bomb: Skin Color, Prejudice, and Intelligence, The* (Ehrlich and Feldman), 82
*Race: a Study in Modern Superstition* (Barzun), xi, 55
Racial/ethnic classifications, 94, 104, 107, 138–139
Racial/ethnic headcounts, 104–107, 113–115, 132, 135, 138–139
Racial/ethnic origins, 107–115, 118
Rogers, J. A., 59–60, 80, 129

*Schools of Shaker Heights; everyone a winner! The*, 103–106
School System Summary Report, 107–115, 135, 139
*Sex and Race* (Rogers), 60

Shaker Heights Housing Office, 123–124
Shaker Heights interracial relations workshop, 121–123
Shaker Heights schools plan, 124, 131–132
*Shaker Heights School Review*, 131–132
*Simple Takes a Wife* (Hughes), 9
*Story of John Hope, The* (Torrence), 47, 50

Torrence, Ridgely, 49, 50

U.S. Commission on Civil Rights, 127
U.S. Department of Commerce, 91, 102
U.S. Department of Education, 107–108, 113, 135, 139
U.S. Supreme Court, 44, 141

Washington, Joseph, 112
"Webster," 142
White, definition of, 108–109, 111
White flight, 126–129
White liberals, 127–129
White purity, 43–45, 59, 101, 110–111, 114–115
White, Walter, vii, 45–47, 52

Zabel, William, 112